FEMINISM
AND
CHRISTIANITY

Abingdon Essential Guides
Editorial Advisory Board

FEMINISM AND CHRISTIANITY

An Essential Guide

Lynn Japinga

ABINGDON PRESS
Nashville

FEMINISM AND CHRISTIANITY:
AN ESSENTIAL GUIDE

Copyright © 1999 by Abingdon Press

This book is printed on recycled, acid-free paper.

Library of Congress Cataloging-in-Publication Data

Japinga, Lynn, 1960-
  Feminism and Christianity: an essential guide   /   Lynn Japinga.
    p.   cm.—(Abingdon essential guides)
  Includes bibliographical references (p.   ).
  ISBN 0-687-07760-5 (alk. paper)
    1. Feminist theology.   I. Title.   II. Series.
  BT83.55 .J37 1999
  230'.082—dc21
                                                      99-049430
                                                      CIP

Scripture quotations, unless otherwise indicated, are from the New Revised Standard Version Bible, copyright © 1989, by the Division of Christian Education of the National Council of the Churches of Christ in the United States of America.

Scripture quotations marked CEV are from the *Contemporary English Version*, copyright © 1991, 1992, 1995 by American Bible Society. Used by permission.

Scripture quotations marked KJV are from the King James Version of the Bible.

99 00 01 02 03 04 05 06 07 08 — 10 9 8 7 6 5 4 3 2 1

MANUFACTURED IN THE UNITED STATES OF AMERICA

Contents

Acknowledgments

When I was awarded tenure and submitted this manuscript to the publishers, my husband, who was even more relieved than I, commissioned a painting from artist Elizabeth DeBraber. The painting depicts a woman walking out of a forest, carrying a book. Embroidered into the folds of her dress are the names of the women in my family, several of the feminist theologians who have most influenced me, and several of my friends. It is a stunning work, and it reminds me of the ways our lives are woven together. The painting celebrates strong women, friendship, family, and scholarship.

The feminist theologians represented in this book, and many others who are not explicitly named, have demonstrated creativity and courage. Their work and ideas are only briefly summarized in this book, but their influence upon my thinking and upon the academic study of religion is extensive and profound.

Three student assistants worked with me at various stages of the research. Ann Verhey-Henke, Anne Lucas, and Jodi Ten Harkel tracked down sources, reviewed literature, and made helpful suggestions on early drafts. Their enthusiasm, good humor, and organizational skills were invaluable.

A number of people read drafts at various stages. Diane Maodush-Pitzer, Jeanne Jacobson, Cathleen Jaworowski, Sandy Hansen, Anna Cook, Marla Lunderberg, Bette Williams, Cindi Veldheer-DeYoung, Jennifer Adams, Kurt Dershem, and Jeff Japinga offered constructive comments and good conversation.

My students have always taught me about teaching, about life, and about courage. I appreciate their insights, their efforts, and their criticisms. They have made the classroom a joyful place to be.

Several friends provided moral support and prodding to finish. Renee House, E. Elizabeth Johnson, Kathryn Roberts, Kama Jongerius

Zuidema, Deirdre Johnston, Jane Dickie, Jane Bach, Robert Baird, Robert Klouw, and Dennis TeBeest offered encouragement and laughter. My parents and in-laws, Roger and Wilma Winkels, and Norm and Shirley Japinga, frequently cared for our children and did numerous other tasks that made my life easier.

Hope College provided several summer grants and reduced teaching loads. My colleagues in the Department of Religion set high standards for scholarship and teaching, and it is a privilege to work with them. Karen Michmerhuizen patiently solved computer problems, made corrections, and managed footnotes. Donald Luidens and Roger Nemeth graciously allowed me to postpone work on a joint project so that I could finish this book.

My family, Jeff, Mark, and Annie, has been good-humored about the time I have spent at my desk. They also offered many interesting interruptions. To them I offer my deep gratitude for the joy they bring to my life.

Holland, Michigan
September 1999

Introduction

On the facade of a church in Rome is a statue of a woman lying on the ground with a man standing above her, his foot placed firmly on her neck. A photograph of the statue hangs in the study of a friend of mine, next to a letter she received from the governing body of her home church. The letter informed her that although they recognized her abilities, they would not recommend her for a college religion department scholarship because women should not be ministers.

It is an experience many women have had. In 1837, for example, Sarah Grimke gave a series of lectures encouraging the abolition of slavery. The lectures caused quite a stir, not only for their content, but because conventional wisdom claimed that a woman who expressed her opinion before a group of men and women endangered both herself and the audience. The Congregationalist clergy of Massachusetts issued a pastoral letter condemning Grimke for entering public life and abandoning the rightful sphere to which she had been assigned by God. Sarah Grimke responded with a series of letters, including one that reads:

Woman I am aware stands charged to the present day with having brought sin into the world. I shall not repel the charge by any counter assertions, although, as was before hinted, Adam's ready acquiescence with his wife's proposal, does not savor much of that superiority in strength of mind, which is arrogated by man. Even admitting that Eve was the greater sinner, it seems to me man might be satisfied with the dominion he has claimed and exercised for nearly six thousand years, and that more true nobility would be manifested by endeavoring to raise the fallen and invigorate the weak, than by keeping woman in subjection. But I ask no favors for my sex. I surrender not our claim to equality. All I ask of our

9

brethren is that they will take their feet from off our necks and permit us to stand upright on that ground which God designed us to occupy.[1]

For centuries some women have had an ambivalent relationship with religion, particularly with Christianity. They wonder how a tradition values and affirms women when its central figures, God the Father, Jesus the Son, the twelve apostles, and a host of other prophets, priests, and kings, are all male. They wonder where the good news is in biblical texts about women who are raped, murdered, ignored, or valued primarily for their wombs. They point to quotations from the church "fathers" that blame women for human sin or claim that a woman is a misbegotten or defective male. They note that some contemporary churches do not permit women to serve as priests or pastors; and if women are ordained to the ministry, they are often denied positions of power and influence. Many feminists have dismissed Christianity as hopelessly male centered and biased against women. Those who have not dismissed Christianity suspect that it has helped to create a society that does not consider women and men to be equally gifted and valuable.

Christians have been no less skeptical of feminists. Some Christians have accused feminists of being selfish, trying to take over the world, and reversing all roles so that women will be able to dominate men. Feminists want to deny all differences between men and women, critics say; they want to destroy the traditional family and force all women to work outside the home and all children to attend day care. Feminists do not believe in the Bible or God, and they want to undermine the influence of Christianity.

As you read these critiques you may be protesting, "But that isn't what Christianity is all about," or "Feminists don't believe that!" And that is exactly the problem. Both Christians and feminists have often dealt with each other on the basis of stereotypes, half-truths, and caricatures. The popular media has encouraged this misunderstanding. More Americans have heard the term "femi-nazi" than have heard a thoughtful definition of feminism.

I teach in a private, church-related liberal arts college; and I am always a bit taken aback by the number of students, especially women, who refuse to identify themselves as feminists because the term has negative connotations. Feminists, they tell me, are angry, they do not wear makeup, they are always complaining about something, and they hate men. Female students assume that they have the right to an education, the right to a job or to a slot in graduate school, the right to enter a male-dominated profession, and the right to equal wages. They have reaped the benefits of the feminist movement, but know little of its history and do not want to be identified with it. They do not fully realize that forty years ago women were not considered viable candidates for graduate schools or the professions because their primary role was to bear and rear children. Women have more choices now because of the efforts of women who have gone before us.

Feminism, as it arose in the nineteenth century and in its more recent manifestations, emphasizes power, rights, and freedom from oppression. How, then, does Christianity, with its emphasis on self-sacrifice and turning the other cheek, fit into this discussion? Many of the students in my Christian Feminism course wonder how Christianity and feminism can be compatible. Isn't Christian feminism an oxymoron?

Feminism and Christianity

Although the feminist movement that arose in the last half of the twentieth century did not begin in a church, as did the feminist movement of the mid-nineteenth century, Christianity and feminism began to intersect fairly quickly during this period. In 1968 Mary Daly, professor of theology and philosophy at Boston College, published a book entitled *The Church and the Second Sex,* in which she described the Roman Catholic Church's failure to treat women as equal human beings. More damaging than the Catholic Church's restriction of the priesthood to males, she argued, is the belief that women are more at fault for sin and that their God-given nature requires them to be secondary—the supportive, nurturing, submissive partner in marriage and church. Five years later Daly published *Beyond God the Father,* charging that most Christian doctrines are hopelessly male centered and misogynistic.

Even if they did not read Daly or belong to the Roman Catholic Church, some Christian women began to question their roles in ecclesiastical structures and their place within Christian theology. The Bible, they said, presents at best an ambiguous picture of women. In the Old Testament, women were valued primarily for their reproductive capacity. Their menstrual cycles made women ritually unclean for two weeks each month. Women often resorted to deception or manipulation to exert influence over their husbands or children. Yet the Old Testament also speaks of strong women who were instrumental in the well-being of the nation. Shiphrah and Puah, Miriam, Deborah, Ruth, and Rahab are examples of positive female role models in the Old Testament.

The New Testament was equally ambivalent. The apostle Paul told women to keep silent in church, but earlier in the same letter he told women to cover their heads appropriately when they spoke in church.

Jesus never ordained women to church office,[2] but he treated them with respect and care, and he broke many religious rules to do so.

Biblical scholars, such as Elisabeth Schüssler Fiorenza and Phyllis Trible, began writing powerful and profound treatments of various biblical texts. Schüssler Fiorenza argued that the scattered biblical references to women in the early church were only the tip of the iceberg and that women led and influenced the early church in many ways.

Women who began to study the history of Christianity found a similar mixture of bad news and good news. The church fathers had much to say about women, and most of it was negative or critical. In the fourth century Augustine argued that women were not created in the image of God, but only in relationship to their husbands. Men, on the other hand, fully represented the image of God by themselves. Women were useful for childbearing, Augustine wrote, but otherwise a man made the better friend and companion. The thirteenth-century theologian Thomas Aquinas claimed that women were misbegotten males, the result of a defective process of conception.

While the fathers wondered whether women were fully human, they knew for certain that women were fully sinful. Late in the second century the theologian Tertullian wrote: "Woman, you are the devil's doorway. It is your fault that the Son of Man has to die." Could women be fully redeemed from the effects of their sin? The fathers were not sure. Eve's sin in eating the fruit in the garden meant that women could not be entrusted with leadership. Women were considered dangerous temptresses who needed to be controlled.

Again, in the midst of all this bad news, there were stories of women who contributed to the well-being of the church: Mary the mother of Jesus, Mary Magdalene, Phoebe, and Priscilla in the New Testament; Perpetua, Macrina, Julian of Norwich, and Catherine of Siena in the years that followed the New Testament period. Some wielded a great deal of influence upon church and society.

Finally, Christian feminists began reexamining traditional Christian doctrines, particularly the belief that God is most clearly represented through male language and imagery. Mary Daly's pithy phrase, "If God is male, then the male is God," offered a stinging critique of father language. But in addition to such critiques, feminist theologians have explored a variety of biblical images and metaphors that say something true about God.

Christian feminists, like feminists of other faiths or nonreligious feminists, represent a range of positions. Evangelical feminists tend to be more conservative in their attempts to preserve traditional Christian doctrines. They affirm the authority of the Bible and its continuing relevance to human lives. At the other end of the spectrum, some feminists no longer identify themselves as Christian because they believe Christianity degrades women and encourages their subordination. There are many positions in the middle of this spectrum. Many Christian feminists are affiliated with the Roman Catholic Church or with Protestant denominations such as the Episcopal, United Methodist, and Presbyterian churches. A number of influential Christian feminist voices have come from womanist (African American), *mujerista* (Hispanic), and Asian American theologians.

These Christian feminists do not have identical opinions about the Bible, the church, or even Christianity; but most would agree on a basic definition of feminism as a commitment to the humanity, dignity, and equality of all persons. They seek equal rights for women, but their ultimate goal is a social order in which women and men of all races and classes can live together in justice and harmony. Most Christian feminists agree that two tasks or strategies are necessary to achieve this goal.

The first task is resistance to everything that oppresses human beings. This means saying no to sexism, domination, unequal treatment, and injustice. Resistance includes a diagnosis and critique of patriarchal social structures and ideologies. Although this task often prompts the criticism that feminists are angry or hostile, resistance stems from a desire to create a positive, supportive environment for women and men by clearing away what has been hurtful and restrictive in their lives. In Sarah Grimke's words, resistance is asking the brothers to take their feet off women's necks.

The second task of feminism is to empower and encourage women by helping them to find inner strength, a clear sense of identity, and freedom from stereotypes. Feminism recognizes the importance of women's stories and the need to find examples of strength and courage in both the past and the present. Feminism affirms the many and varied gifts of women, both the traditional ones of bearing and rearing children, teaching, nurturing, and the like, but also the more recently recognized gifts of women in administration, leadership, ministry, and the professions. Although their stories are seldom told, women of all races and classes have been a force in history, and their contributions deserve recognition.

Many feminists, whether Christian or not, might agree on the preceding definition and strategies. A particularly Christian approach to feminism might add that the source for these beliefs about dignity and equality is the theological assertion that all people are created in God's image and therefore are valuable, gifted, free, and responsible. Human relationships have been marred by sin; but the sexism, racism, and classism present in our world are not God's will, but signs of brokenness

God is working to transform. God calls humanity to share in the process of transformation of the world, not because we can create a utopia, but because we can make a difference in the institutions, neighborhoods, churches, and families where we work and live.

Christian feminist theology is a rapidly expanding field of study; and many creative, thoughtful, and challenging books are being written by feminist theologians. The intention of this book is not to offer new ideas about feminism so much as to interpret the existing feminist proposals for people who may be new to feminism or theology. This book introduces students to the central themes of Christian feminism and its critiques of traditional Christian doctrines. It is representative and suggestive rather than comprehensive, but I hope it will whet the reader's appetite for more reading, study, and learning.

A simple, but powerful, song from the civil rights movement repeated these words: "We who believe in freedom cannot rest, we who believe in freedom cannot rest until it comes." That is what Christian feminism is about. Freedom for all persons, not just for middle-class white women, but for all women and men. Freedom to do God's work. Freedom to live without destructive stereotypes. Freedom to value women's stories as much as we value men's. Freedom to "stand upright on that ground which God designed us to occupy."

Both Christians and feminists have asked if it is possible to be both a Christian and a feminist. I ask the question a bit differently. Is it possible not to be?

CHAPTER 1

An Introduction to Feminist Theology

How many theologians can you name who wrote before 1950? Even if you are not very familiar with the history of Christianity, you have probably encountered Augustine in a world literature class, Aquinas in a history class, and Jonathan Edwards in American literature. Now, how many *women* theologians can you name? Even those students who have attended Sunday school all their lives or attended a religious private school may have difficulty generating a short list of women theologians. Perhaps "women theologians" is an oxymoron like "Christian feminism." Perhaps there were no women who wrote theology. Or perhaps there were many such women, but we do not know about them.

Mary Magdalene was a faithful disciple who went to the tomb of Jesus on Easter morning and found it empty. In three of the four gospels she is named as one of the first to see and speak to Jesus. The early church recognized her as a person of insight and influence, but Paul did not include her in his list of witnesses to the resurrection (1 Corinthians 15:5-8). She became identified as a prostitute, although there is no biblical evidence for that reputation. Today we know her not as a theologian and a witness to the resurrection, but as a sinful woman redeemed by the compassion of Jesus.

Martha of Bethany, in the midst of grief over the death of her brother Lazarus, recognized the power of Jesus to heal and to bring new life and named him as the Messiah, the Son of God (John 11:17-27). Later the disciple Peter made a similar confession (Matt 16:16; Mark 8:29; Luke 9:20) and was rewarded with a particular place of leadership. Martha, however, is remembered almost exclusively as a fussy homemaker who scolded her sister Mary for listening to Jesus while Martha did all of the work (Luke 10:38-42).

Perpetua was a young woman killed because of her faith during a time of persecution at the end of the second century. For a number of years her theological reflections were read in public worship, but eventually they were replaced by the statements of important men who had died as martyrs. Only recently have her powerful words been recovered.

Paula was a wealthy woman and the mother of five children. After her husband died late in the fourth century, she felt called to study Scripture and to devote herself to the things of God. She excelled in Hebrew and founded monastic communities along with her friend and fellow scholar, Jerome. Paula was respected for her deep piety, strict asceticism, and obvious intellectual and administrative abilities; but she could not be considered a teacher of the church, as Jerome was. Despite the extent of her influence and the depth of her wisdom, her writings were not considered important enough to preserve.

Julian of Norwich (1342–1416) spent much of her life in a small cell attached to a church in Norwich, England. During an illness when she was thirty years old, she had a series of visions in which she encountered God in profound ways; and she spent much of the remainder of her life meditating on these visions. Like other mystics of her time, she used feminine imagery to describe God and Jesus. She wrote, "As truly as God is our Father, so truly is God our Mother. Our Father wills, our Mother works, our good Lord the Holy Spirit confirms. And therefore it is our part to love our God in whom we have our being, reverently thanking and praising him for our creation, mightily praying to our Mother for mercy and pity, and to our Lord the Holy Spirit for help and grace."[1] Julian's work was preserved, but the church has only recently begun to grapple with the implications of her theological insights.

Anne Hutchinson was a gifted teacher and theologian in Boston in the 1630s. As a leader of Bible studies for women, she explained the sermon delivered the previous Sunday. Soon dozens of men attended as well. The Puritan leaders feared her influence and disapproved of her ideas, especially the heretical notion that God might presume to speak directly to a woman. As a result of her independence, influence and insight, Anne was banished from Massachusetts.

Sojourner Truth (1795–1883) was born into slavery but was freed in 1827. She spent much of her life fighting for the rights of women and African Americans. She could not read or write, but she learned Scripture by having children read the Bible to her. In 1851 she attended a women's rights convention in Akron, Ohio, where some clergymen claimed that women should not have equal rights because they lacked sufficient intellect, because Eve caused sin, and because Christ was a man. She refuted the last argument by asking, "Where did your Christ come from? From God and a woman! Man had nothing to do with him." She displayed extraordinary courage both in refuting the arguments of the clergy despite her minimal education and by speaking up when many of the women present did not want a black woman to speak and possibly endanger their cause. Her speech had an electrifying effect on the crowd, and today students who read it still find it deeply moving.

How much truth and insight has been lost over two thousand years of Christian history because the theological wisdom of women has not been recognized, appreciated, or recorded? For centuries only celibate women had full freedom to study, write, and devote themselves to God and the church. What contributions might wives and mothers have made? Would theology be different today if the church had recognized women's gifts throughout its history? What has the church lost by refusing to hear the voices of women?

One of the most important tasks of feminist theology is first to recover and listen to the voices of women who have spoken in the past, but have been silenced or forgotten or dismissed as heretical; and second, to encourage and attend to contemporary women's voices. Feminist theology asks how the Christian tradition might be different if it listened to women's voices. This chapter will explore theoretical questions about the definitions of theology and feminist theology; the methods feminist theologians use to do their work; and some of their assumptions, emphases, and goals.

What is Theology?

The most basic definition of theology is thinking about God, which comes from the Greek words *theos* (God) and *logos* (words or thought). Theology is usually understood more broadly as reflection about God, humanity, and the world, including the topics of anthropology (human nature), christology (Jesus Christ), and ecclesiology (the church). Another helpful definition of theology is faith seeking understanding, or the attempt to make sense of, interpret and articulate what it is we believe.

Traditional definitions of theology stress its rational, objective character. Theological works like John Calvin's *Institutes of the Christian Religion* or Thomas Aquinas' *Summa Theologiae* present the content of the Bible and the Christian tradition in an organized, systematic form. These authors attempt to explain, simply and systematically, the truth of the Christian faith, or as it is sometimes phrased, they are "thinking God's thoughts after him." The assumption that such theological reflection springs forth complete and inerrant from the mind of God through the pen of a particular theologian like Calvin on Aquinas gives theologians enormous power. If Aquinas was simply setting forth the truth of the Christian faith, then it is difficult to disagree. If Calvin is an objective and unbiased interpreter of Christianity, a lesser mind should not presume to criticize. Certainly Calvin and Aquinas were skilled theologians, but they were also human.

Many Christians have never fully recognized that even the most abstract theology develops out of the experience of the theologian. John Calvin's *Institutes of the Christian Religion* are often regarded as a model of disengaged, pure theology, but they arose out of Calvin's passionate desire to articulate the Protestant faith in a hostile context. His personality, legal training and ecclesiastical agenda are evident on every page.

In recent years some Christians have questioned the assumption that theology is rational, objective, and free of bias. Thinking and writing about God cannot be separated from the life of the theologian. A person who has experienced God as angry and judgmental will write differently than a person who has found God to be gracious and loving. A middle-class, tenured professor will have a different sense of God's provision than a poor coffee bean picker in Central America. A man who is certain he is created in God's image will have a different sense of God than a woman who has been taught that she is one step removed from the image of God.

Theology can be shaped by the economic status, job security, childhood, gender, race, and life story of the author. Martin Luther, whose theological and biblical reflections shape the identity of the Lutheran churches nearly five centuries later, agonized as a young man over his relationship to God and to the church. He lamented his failure to be good enough or do enough to earn God's approval. Out of this pain and his joyful experience of God's forgiveness, he seized upon the biblical concept of justification by grace through faith. The encounter with divine grace freed him from compulsively seeking to please God, but also made him critical of anything he felt corrupted the heart of the gospel. Luther wrote passionate treatises against the church's attempt to sell forgiveness in the form of indulgences or to dole out grace through the sacraments. Theology for Luther was not objective, but an effort to protect the grace of God from human manipulation. His energy and insight came not from dispassionate academic study, but from wrestling with the questions that were most significant to his life and faith.

When theologians speak honestly about their own experience, it need not comprise the integrity of their work. The greater danger arises when theologians assume that their work simply reflects the truth and will of God. In the nineteenth century a catechism for slaves asked the question, "Why was I created?" and answered, "To serve my master." To a white Southerner, this theology expressed the will of God; but to an abolitionist, it denied God's intention for the dignity of all humanity; and to a slave, it represented oppression wearing pious clothes. Simply labeling one's ideas "theology" does not guarantee that they represent the mind of God.

Theology does not finally represent the mind of God so much as it illustrates the efforts of human beings to gain a deeper understanding of God, themselves, and the world. Theology is not abstract and objective, but arises out of human lives, conflicts, doubts and dreams.

Why Feminist Theology?

When theology is understood as faith seeking understanding, it becomes clear that people's approach to theology will differ depending on the questions they ask and the areas in which they seek clarity. Martin Luther asked how people became acceptable to God. John Calvin wondered how God cared for and guided the world. The most pressing question for many feminist theologians is whether the Christian faith can be a positive force in women's lives when it says so much that is negative about women.

Having recognized the unfair treatment of women and been angered by it, many feminists began to see the world differently. Perhaps they noticed the sexist language in a hymn or in liturgy and realized that they did not feel included. Perhaps they were denied the opportunity to do something because of gender. Perhaps they heard someone talk about sexism and had a flash of insight that they were not alone in their discomfort with the church or with society.

For some women the experience of inclusion helps them to realize how much they have missed. Carter Heyward received a letter from a woman who participated in a communion service Heyward led soon after her ordination. The woman wrote:

> I did not expect to be so personally affected by your presence here. I was unaware of the ways that I have felt excluded from God's inner circle of love until I experienced being included—both by the obvious fact of your inclusion and by you, as God's representative, including me. *Somehow I feel I've spent my life trying to be God's son, only to realize at last that I am God's daughter.*[2]

Once women recognize and begin to resist exclusion, they find that they see the world quite differently. Regina Coll described her experience:

> After my own conversion to feminism, when I read scripture I often said, "That's new; it wasn't there the last time. Someone must have sneaked it in when I wasn't looking." Of course, it was always there. I had been unseeing. I had read the words from the perspective of the culture in which I lived and understood them from that perspective. But when my world-view changed, so did my ability to vision and revision scripture (and incidentally to revise and revision *The New York Times*, television shows, and the theater). I was left with questions, surprises, and disappointments. The new view was not always comforting.[3]

Once changed, most women find that they cannot go back to the way they were. They cannot eliminate feminist consciousness once it has developed. Mary Daly wrote of this experience: "Seeing means that everything changes: the old identifications and the old securities are gone."[4] Once women (and men) notice the presence of exclusive language in a worship service, it is almost impossible to return to blissful oblivion. Once women ask if they are included in the hymn "Rise Up, O Men of God," they can never sing it without wondering. The development of feminist consciousness produces a paradigm shift for many women. They begin to look at the world in a different way, and all aspects of their lives are affected.[5]

Women who ask these questions about exclusion and equality find that the traditional theological answers do not always satisfy them. The insistence on the fatherhood of God, the claim that women brought sin into the world, and the exclusion of women from the church and the priesthood make it difficult for women to accept the Christian tradition uncritically. Some feminists reject Christianity at this point as hopelessly patriarchal and unredeemable. Others choose to stay in the Christian tradition, but continue to struggle with its pervasive sexism. Feminist theologians seek to understand and make sense of this ambiguous Christian faith, which both affirms women as God's people and excludes them from the life of the church. Many feminist theologians believe that ultimately the Christian faith does offer good news to women, but not without some hard work at sorting through the meaning of the tradition for them.

Feminist theology begins with the assumption that women are fully human, made in God's image, and loved and valued by God. Rosemary

Radford Ruether described three tasks of feminist theology arising out of this starting point. First, feminist theology provides a critique of the tradition, pointing out the ways the Christian tradition has been limiting or destructive for women. Second, it tries to recover women's stories from the past and the present in order to demonstrate the gifts and insights of women throughout history. It explores the ways women have done theology. Third, feminist theology revisions and reshapes traditional Christian doctrines and practices in order to help the tradition and the church to be more responsive to the needs and experiences of all its members.[6]

Feminist theologians also challenge some of the common beliefs about how theology ought to be done and by whom. Theology is not a top-down enterprise in which brilliant scholars tell ordinary Christians the truth about God. Theology is not the exclusive property of persons with academic degrees and clergy credentials, but the task of all Christians who wonder about God, themselves, and the world. Theology arises more out of curiosity than certainty. It is not so much a setting forth of absolute truth as a setting forth of the ways in which God is present in human lives. Theology is not confined to rational exposition in textbooks or sermons, but can be found in novels, poetry, art, and music. Theological insight can be found in all forms of expression that help people encounter God.

Feminist theologians also insist that theology is not meant to be a dry, abstract debate about irrelevant and esoteric topics. Critics sometimes charge that feminist theologians make too great a fuss about theological issues because, after all, it does not matter what we call God or how we define sin. Feminist theologians reply that these issues matter a great deal because they are speaking of the holy and of human lives. Roberta Bondi wrote that theology is important because it is about saving lives.

> First, [theology] involves learning to see the ways in which false images of God, ourselves, and the world have bound us and taken away the life God intends for us. Second, it involves learning to know God as God is, as a healing God, and learning to know ourselves, individually and communally, as people who correspond with that God in whose image we are made. Third, it involves imagining a future that is consistent with the God we come to know.[7]

Theology at its best is a life-giving enterprise. One of the significant insights of feminist psychologists is the need for girls and women to develop their own voice, to be comfortable speaking, even disagreeing, without feeling that they must keep quiet in order to preserve their relationships and their security. Certain aspects of the Christian tradition have discouraged women from this task of finding their voices, by commanding their silence or by saying that "good Christian women" are not disagreeable. Feminist theology attempts to give women both life and voice.

Giving Voice to Women Through Critique of the Tradition

The chapters that follow will identify some of the pronouncements and practices in the Christian tradition that have been especially harmful or restrictive for women. More subtle, but no less damaging, are the ways women have been excluded, ignored, or dismissed. Chung Hyun Kyung called this "the violence of silence."[8] Traditional theology has been written by men, for men, about men. Women always have to ask how they are included, if at all. Women's experience has been ignored or neglected in the doing of theology, as if they do not exist or are an afterthought. The Christian tradition has valued women as wives, mothers, or virgins, but rarely for their intellect, vocation, or contribution to society. Women have had neither the freedom to choose nor the choices men have assumed were a part of being human.

The reasons often given to justify these attitudes is that they are taught by the Bible and the Christian tradition and that the church's past thought, speech, and action ought to determine contemporary expressions of faith. Change defies God's will and threatens the essence of the gospel. If the Nicene Creed, written in the fourth century, said that "Jesus became man for us men and our salvation," the church must use that language without complaint. If the church has never ordained women to the priesthood, it should not start now.

This interpretation of tradition has made the Christian faith very difficult for women. The content of the tradition is difficult enough, but the tradition itself has become cloaked in an aura of sanctity and unchangeability. Feminist theologians have refused to accept the tradition, simply because it is tradition, as the absolute will of God for the present.

Skepticism about tradition does not mean that feminist theologians discard all tradition as worthless or throw out the entire history and faith of the church and create a new religion. Their approach is not unlike that of stripping furniture, removing the layers of old paint to find what kind of wood lies underneath. Most feminist theologians ask hard questions of the tradition in order to assess the author's assumptions, the attitudes of his culture about the nature of women, and the personal experiences that shaped his theological beliefs.

Thomas Aquinas, a thirteenth-century theologian, wrote that women were defective beings, born female because an environmental factor had determined their sex in the womb. He learned biology from Aristotle, a philosopher from the fourth century before Christ who believed that a male sperm contained within it a tiny person that would grow into another male if all went well and if there was no humid wind from the south. Aristotle and Aquinas believed that the mother simply provided the proper environment. They did not know then that a sperm and an egg are required for conception or that an individual's sex depends on chromosomes, not on the weather. Unfortunately, Aquinas concluded from this that women were defective, inferior, and unfit for the intellectual and administrative demands of the priesthood. His ideas shaped the Roman Catholic Church's understanding of men and women. Although modern biology has provided more accurate knowledge of procreation, the theological conclusions based on this ancient model have not changed. Aquinas's argument is still used to deny the priesthood to women.

Augustine was a theologian in the fourth century who struggled with the sin of lust both before and after his conversion to Christianity. In his writings he argued that sexual activity before the Fall was a matter of the will, not of passion. He advised Christians to be cautious about their sexuality and spoke at length about its dangers. His opinions have also had a significant impact on theology and practice in the Christian tradition, even though his view was more negative than that of the Bible.

Jerome was an ascetic and a scholar in the fourth century and a friend and advisor to Paula. He wrote a treatise on the virtue of virginity, dedicated to one of Paula's daughters, in which he described the disgusting nature of sexuality and childbirth and concluded that the only good thing about marriage was that a couple could produce children to raise as virgins for the service of the church. He wrote in a time when asceticism or self-denial were seen as the most valuable ways to prove one's commitment to God.

Some feminists have concluded that this Christian tradition is patriarchal to the core. Daphne Hampson claimed that when God, Christ, priests, saints, and symbols are all male, the Christian faith cannot function positively for women. Mary Daly arrived at a similar conclusion when she moved "beyond God the Father" and labeled herself post-Christian. She maintained that the tradition was developed by men in part as a way to preserve their power. The church fathers invoke tradition as an absolute, which eliminates the possibility of dialogue. Daly argued that women are not bound to obey such a harmful tradition, and she encouraged women to decide for themselves what is true and not seek justification in the past for their beliefs.[9]

Other feminist theologians believe that although the church fathers had a significant impact on the church's view of women and sexuality, their ideas do not represent the mind of God for all time. The tradition helps contemporary Christians understand and learn from the ways the church has dealt with theological issues, but the answers of the past do not determine how Christians should think and act today.[10] The tradition can be adapted as necessary to make it relevant to contemporary theology. Ivone Gebara wrote that tradition need not be repeated for perpetuity without change or challenge. "If we do repeat, it is because that is what today's situation demands, because it does touch the roots of our existence, because to some extent it responds to the problems that ongoing history sets before us. In this sense, what is normative is primarily the present, what calls out today; tradition is viewed in terms of the present."[11] Christians need not be bound to the tradition.

Some feminist theologians remain within the tradition by identifying particular aspects that represent the essence or core of the gospel, such as the words of the prophets, the teachings of Jesus, or a principle implicit in Scripture, although not stated explicitly. Rosemary Radford Ruether outlined her criteria for evaluating the Christian tradition:

> The critical principle of feminist theology is the promotion of the full humanity of women. Whatever denies, diminishes, or distorts the full humanity of women is, therefore, appraised as not redemptive. Theologically speaking, whatever diminishes or denies the full humanity of women must be presumed not to reflect the divine or an authentic relation to the divine, or to reflect the authentic nature of things, or to be the message or work of an authentic redeemer or a community of redemption. This negative principle also implies the positive principle: what does promote the full humanity of women is of the Holy, it does reflect true relation to the divine, it is the true nature of things, the authentic message of redemption and the mission of redemptive community.[12]

This means that texts that tell women to be submissive and silent and theological treatises and papal statements that insist that women cannot be priests are not authentic messages of redemption because they do not promote the full humanity of women. A text in which Jesus encouraged the Samaritan woman to preach to her neighbors (John 4) or the insights of the mystics who experience God and Christ in feminine images are authentic messages of redemption because they promote the full humanity of women.

Critics have argued that these criteria are too narrow because they enable feminist theologians to disregard a large portion of the Christian tradition simply because it does not help women to flourish. These critics charge that feminists impose the secular agenda of equality upon the tradition and do not take seriously enough the timeless truths of the Christian faith. Rather than simply accepting and obeying the teachings of Jesus, these critics contend, feminist theologians presume to use their own values as a test for the validity of Scripture and tradition instead of allowing their values and commitments to be shaped by the Christian faith.

Feminists respond that the culture as a whole has not consistently advocated equal treatment for all people. Equality has not been the dominant theme in a culture where racism, sexism, classism, and other forms of discrimination are present in all social institutions. When certain groups of people or institutions oppress other groups, they presume to decide the value and worth of other human beings simply on the basis of race, gender, class, and sexual orientation, without considering individual gifts and interests. People who are oppressed in these ways often internalize these judgments and agree that they are capable of performing only the particular roles in life that have been assigned to them. The resistance to oppression that feminists advocate is not simply a way to improve their own social location or to achieve a few more rights for themselves; it is, rather, a way to enable all of God's people to live in the freedom and justice God intends for them. Feminist theologians believe that the tradition needs to be called to account when it denies God's people the dignity, compassion, and justice Jesus and the prophets mandated.

Finally, the feminist critique of tradition emphasizes that theology is a partial, fallible attempt to say something true and meaningful about the God who transcends all human understanding. Human knowledge is incomplete and at times distorted, which means that human efforts at theology are never complete, but always in process. Aurelia Fule, a Presbyterian minister and theologian, observed: "If we believe we have arrived and are no longer traveling toward the truth, we have become unformable in God's hands and unteachable in our hearts."[13] Feminist theologians assert that all theologians, including themselves, need to be humble about the theological enterprise. This means that beliefs are stated with a caution that recognizes that no human being can be absolutely right when making statements about God. Humility is an awareness that God might choose to act in ways that defy the best theories, the recognition that the surprising work of God is not yet finished and that at the end of life human beings may be stunned by the grace of God. Neither the tradition nor contemporary theologians fully understand God, and neither should be viewed as infallible, but always open to deeper understanding and insight.

Giving Voice to Women by Telling Their Stories

When my students first encounter the stories of women in the history of Christianity or American religion, the most common response is, "I've never heard that before." They are amazed at the existence of these strong and courageous women and wonder why they were never mentioned in history books or Sunday school.

A quick overview of the history of the church shows mostly men serving as priests, church leaders, theologians, reformers, social activists, and mystics. The index to a typical history of Christianity includes only a few women's names, but the fact that women rarely appear in the history books does not mean they had no role in the church. There are women in many of these categories; there is even a story about a woman pope. Why has so little been recorded about women?

Historians have often assumed that women did not do anything. They were wives and mothers who did not contribute to the theological task because they were not educated and therefore did not write or think deep thoughts. If they did have opinions they probably agreed with their husbands and therefore provided nothing new to write about.

It is often true that the winners write history and decide how to tell the story of the disagreement and how to present the other side. Mary Magdalene's reputation as a prostitute may have arisen from those who felt she was becoming too influential and wanted to limit her power by giving her a bad reputation. In the second century two women, Priscilla and Maximilla, held leadership responsibilities among a group of people known as Montanists, who emphasized the second coming of Jesus and the work of the Holy Spirit. The group was eventually declared heretical, and the women were dismissed as fanatical. This permitted the "orthodox" parts of the church to continue the claim that women never led religious movements.

Theologian Sandra Schneiders has pointed out that history is not the objective and complete rendering of past events that we often assume it to be, but is, rather, the selection of events the historian considers important. "Church history is not the history of the church but of what men have preserved of male experience for male purposes."[14] Since men wrote history, men determined the topics worthy of preservation or inclusion, usually wars, politics, and intellectual debates, in which women were permitted little if any role. British author Virginia Woolf recalled some research she had undertaken for a lecture titled "Women and Fiction." She went to the library of the British Museum, looked up "women" in the catalogue, and was astonished at what she found. "Have you any notion how many books are written about women in the course of one year? Have you any notion how many are written by men? Are you aware that you are, perhaps, the most discussed animal in the universe?"[15] Men had much to say about women, most of it critical, but women seldom wrote about men. Women seldom wrote about any topic, in Woolf's day, partly because they lacked the financial resources and the room of their own that would enable their scholarship.

Throughout much of Christian history women were rarely educated and held few public positions in church, academic, or political life. They worked as craftspersons, brewed beer, made wine, and did all the tasks required to keep a family in food and clothing, which left precious little time for reading and theological reflection. When women did write, their work received scant attention. For centuries women repeated the same arguments and wrestled with the same biblical texts. They did not build on the work of women who came before them because they did not know such work existed; therefore, they did not make as much progress as they might have if they had been able to stand on the shoulders of those who went before them and to build on their arguments.[16]

Given these barriers, it is amazing that any women made significant contributions to the church. An essential task of Christian feminism during the past twenty-five years has been the recovery of women's stories in books such as *Her Story* by Barbara McHaffie, *Daughters of the Church* by Ruth Tucker and Walter Liefeld, *Women of Spirit* edited by Rosemary Radford Ruether and Rosemary Skinner Keller, and a host of others. These historians noted that women have usually constituted half the church membership and sometimes as much as two-thirds. The story of the church is not accurate without considering the role of women. Anne Carr observed, "Less than half the story has been told. To begin to tell the other part is to acknowledge that women have always been involved (even when excluded or ignored) in everything human, in everything religious."[17]

Giving Voice to Women by Valuing Their Experience

Why is it important to tell these stories? Feminist theologians claim that theology and history are incomplete without the experience of women. But if men and women are basically the same, as many feminists claim, what does feminist theology offer that traditional theology does not? Feminist theology claims to be rooted in women's experience, but the meaning of this is often vague. Are women's lives so different from men's lives that they produce a completely different theology? Do women have a distinctive nature that leads them to a feminine version of theology?

Ivone Gebara illustrated some of this ambiguity when she wrote, "There is something quite special in the way that women do theology. The elements of everyday life are very intertwined with their speaking about God. . . . Given their own history, women are bolder in questioning concepts, and they have a creative curiosity that opens new paths and allows new understandings."[18] When feminist theologians refer to women's experience, they are usually thinking of bodily experience, socialized experience, and the experience of oppression or suffering.

First, women's lives are different because their bodies are different. Regular menstrual cycles, pregnancy, childbirth, and breastfeeding are all unique to women. The fact that the body is so prominently involved in much of women's lives has been used to denigrate women, as if these bodily functions limit the development of their brains and souls. One argument against a women president, for example, is that raging hormones would leave her periodically irrational and out of control. Some people believe that women who bear and rear children have little interest or ability in intellectual and cultural issues. Contemporary culture frequently portrays women as attractive objects, valued for their sexuality and beauty, but not for their personalities and minds.

Some feminists assert that women's close connection with the body, particularly the experience of childbirth, makes women less violent, competitive, and judgmental and more compassionate and gracious. Their regular cycles make them more conscious of their bodies, more at home in them, better able to make connections between the mind and the body, and therefore less prone to making war or plundering nature. Because women have often integrated body and soul, they are not trapped by the dualism that divides reality into two opposing categories and elevates one above the other so that the soul and the mind are seen as higher and more important than the body.

How might this bodily experience shape the way women do theology? Feminist theologians insist that sexuality and the body do not need to be transcended by the mind and the spirit or controlled by the will, but may instead provide ways to encounter God. The experiences of pregnancy and childbirth, labeled dirty and disgusting by some theologians, provide several metaphors for thinking about the God in whom we live and move and have our being. Scripture portrays God as a mother laboring to give birth (Isa 42:14) and God as midwife, guiding and encouraging the mother through the birth process (Ps 71:6). Jesus compared his suffering on the cross to the pains of childbirth, which lead to the joy of new life (John 16:21-22).

More broadly, feminist theologians argue that because body and soul are more integrated for women, they are less inclined to see God as a distant Spirit ruling over them. God is not solely concerned with human minds and souls, but with bodies as well. God cares that people have enough to eat, a safe place to sleep, and people with whom they can be in relationship. God cares about all the messy bodily aspects of life.

A second form of women's experience is their socialization. From birth, women have been taught that they are less rational, intelligent, and mathematically gifted than men are. They have been taught, as Henry Higgins sings in *My Fair Lady*, that "Women are irrational, that's all there is to that. Their heads are full of cotton, hay, and rags." Women are good at nurturing and serving others and cleaning up after them, but they are not meant to be leaders or administrators. Women have been told, implicitly and explicitly throughout their lives, that women's work is not as important as men's work, and that girls are not as valuable as boys.

Readers might protest that things have changed and that American society has moved beyond this, but consider these examples. My husband told our daughter that her scribbles looked like a doctor's writing. She announced that women can't be doctors. When I mentioned this to our new woman pediatrician, she said that her daughter had announced that women could be doctors, but only men could be surgeons like her father. Early in their lives children develop clear ideas about what men and women can do, most often through the influence of books, television, and other children; and these ideas persist in adults. When a church that considers itself quite progressive recently called a woman to be the preaching pastor, several parishioners wondered whether a woman would be able to handle the preaching and administrative responsibilities. Feminist theologians suggest that women's experience of inferiority makes them particularly sensitive to the ways inferiority is reinforced in Scripture and in tradition.

A third distinctive characteristic of women's experience is that they are statistically more likely than men to live with suffering, oppression, and poverty. Women earn less money than men and often lose more after a divorce. Women from minority groups and from the Third World may lack adequate food and housing, a basic sense of security, and access to resources. Women often have less power to determine the course of their lives. They are more likely to experience rape, incest, and domestic violence.

Feminist theologians suggest that if theology took the experiences of women into account, it would contain less abstract intellectual debate and more wrestling with concrete issues of survival. In womanist theology, for example, Hagar has become a symbol of suffering. Hagar was a slave owned by Abraham and Sarah. When Sarah did not become pregnant, she gave Hagar to Abraham so that he might conceive a child through her. When Hagar conceived, however, Sarah treated her harshly, and Hagar ran away. Wandering in the wilderness, Hagar encountered God, and the text says that she named God, something no other human did in Scripture. Several years after Ishmael's birth, Sarah sent them away, and Hagar again encountered God when Ishmael nearly died in the wilderness. Womanist theologian Delores Williams has emphasized Hagar's struggle to survive racism and sexism and to ensure her son's well-being.[18] Contrast this, however, to Edith Deen's lengthy comments about Sarah's beauty, faith in God, and deep love for her son Isaac in her book *All the Women of the Bible*. Deen said almost nothing about Hagar's experience, except to criticize her pride. Dean assumed that Sarah's harsh treatment of Hagar was justified because it arose out of Sarah's love for her son.[20]

Giving Voice to Women and Their Diversity

Considering all the emphasis in feminist theology on attending to women's experience, it is painfully ironic that the feminist theology done by white, middle-class, educated women has excluded or at least not paid attention to women who are not white and middle class. In the mid–nineteenth century some white feminists did not want African Americans like Sojourner Truth to be too closely associated with the women's movement, both because of their own racism and because they feared their movement would lose credibility if black women were included. During the suffrage movement some women argued that white middle-class women needed the right to vote in order to balance poorer immigrant men who might not vote the "right" way. In the past few decades the women's movement has worked to obtain opportunities for women in education and the workplace, but has often failed to give much attention to the life and experience of women in minority groups or to the needs of women working in factories, providing day care, or staying at home to care for their own children.

White feminist theology has at times been guilty of overt racism, but most often its racism is more subtle. It has assumed that women are basically the same and that it speaks for all women. At times a feminist theology course might add a single minority woman to its reading list, or a panel discussion might add one woman from a minority group; but such tokenism implies that only one such voice is necessary. Ada Maria Isasi-Diaz, in her book *Mujerista Theology*, pointed out that white feminism did not share power, did not allow Latinas and other minorities to participate in shaping definitions and values, did not deal with issues of race and class, and did not articulate a goal of liberation for all people.[21] When feminist theology does deal with different voices, it is sometimes in a minimal way, at the end of a class or in an optional reading, which implies that these voices are not very important; or it assumes that reading one essay by a minority woman gives adequate insight into the experience of all nonwhite women. In reality, there is no single minority experience; women of all races, classes, and ethnic groups have very diverse stories that cannot be expressed by a single voice.

This criticism of white feminist theology is valid, but it is also true that white feminist theologians have tried to be more inclusive. Rosemary Radford Ruether explored the connections between racism, classism, sexism, and anti-Semitism. Carter Heyward, a white woman, and Katie Geneva Cannon, a black woman, openly explored the dynamics of race in their lives and relationships. Susan Thistlethwaite criticized white feminists for ignoring the insights of nonwhite women. White feminist theologians have begun to encourage their students and readers to attend to more diverse voices.[22]

The attention to diversity can seem a bit overwhelming at times. It is not unusual at an academic conference to have a panel discussion composed of five women of different ethnic groups. Feminist theology is often subdivided into mujerista, womanist, and Asian emphases. It is impossible to make generalizations about women in a particular ethnic group, let alone say anything true about all women. This has been a positive dynamic in feminist theology, but it does pose the question of whether women have any experiences in common. There seems to be little or nothing that unites women from different ages, classes, races, countries, and sexual orientations.

Feminist theologians have encouraged a genuine respect for and engagement with the voices of a wide variety of women. Elizabeth Johnson described the "lens of women's flourishing," as the criterion by which she evaluated theological claims and social structures to determine whether they contribute to the well-being of all women, not just white middle-class women. Feminism will not achieve its goals, she wrote, until the poorest black woman in South Africa is able to live in peace and dignity.[23]

Feminist theologians also encourage greater awareness of diversity. Difference is frightening, and people quickly conclude that different is bad and that someone who looks or thinks differently is inferior. American society has taught that there are limited resources and that if someone else gains, then we must inevitably lose. Feminist theologians propose instead that we will all be enhanced as human beings if we have more exposure to the lives and ideas of those who are different from us.

Giving Voice to Women by Empowering Them

Feminist theologians engage in these tasks of critique, recovery, and revisioning because they hope to empower women and men to live as whole people with thoughts and feelings, bodies and minds, autonomy and relationships, and the confidence that they are valuable human beings. If individuals are to thrive in this way, society must also be transformed. Feminist theologians recognize how enormous the task of social transformation is. They usually are quite realistic about the persistence of sin, but they continue to work so that the world can increasingly become a place that seeks justice and equity and demonstrates respect and care for all its people.

Feminist consciousness tends to be critical or suspicious of the tradition and the status quo. Men have made the rules, and men dominate most of the structures, such as religion, politics, higher education, business, medicine, and law. Even though women are making inroads, men still occupy far more of the tenured faculty, senior staff, bureaucratic, and CEO positions. Men hold a great deal of power and privilege; and women who are allowed into the men's game are expected to play by their rules, work long hours, and publish the same number of articles.

Some people react to such an analysis with concern. "Well, that isn't true," a woman might say. "My husband/father/boyfriend/boss is really wonderful, and he shares the child care or gets his own coffee or helps with the housework." Feminists agree that there are many wonderful men in the world, but individual exceptions do not alter the reality that most structures in our society remain strongly patriarchal and very resistant to change. Consider an institution you are part of—your business, university, or church. Who occupies the top positions? Who holds the power? Who makes the decisions? While there may be a few token women at the top, more than likely it is the men running the show. Other men, while they may not share all of these values and may profess to disagree with a patriarchal system, may still benefit from this "old-boy network."

If transformation and empowerment are to occur, oppression and sexism must first be named and analyzed. Such naming has led to the stereotype that feminists whine and complain about being victimized by sexism. In reality, there is very little self-pity or victim language among feminist theologians. They name the problem and suggest solutions, but they emphasize the strength and abilities of women rather than their weakness and passivity. Naomi Wolf called this "power feminism" as opposed to "victim feminism." Women have abundant wisdom, insight, and intellect. Women should be encouraged to develop identity, courage, and audacity. This emphasis on women's power is often clearest in the writings of Third World feminists, even though they may suffer far more economic and racial exploitation. Ivone Gebara wrote, "Woman is not marked for an unchangeable fate, nor is she the object of alien wills that shape her existence."[24] Despite the difficulties women have experienced over their long history, change is possible.

Change does not come easily, however, so feminist theologians encourage resistance or opposition to what oppresses. It has done little good to hope that structures would change purely out of goodwill because sexism is a power struggle, and those who have power will not easily let go of it. A group of women theologians from the Third World wrote, "Rather than see ourselves solely as victims of male domination, we have formed a sisterhood of resistance to all forms of oppression, seeking creative partnership with men of the Association."[25] Sexism and oppression are deeply embedded in church and society and are very difficult to eradicate. Resistance is more effective if women do it together because they find courage and stamina in their relationships with one another. Feminist theologians find models for resistance in biblical stories in which a woman reached out for healing (Mark 5), a non-Jewish woman had the courage to talk back to Jesus (Mark 7), and two Jewish midwives refused to obey orders to kill the male children of their people (Exodus 1).

Resistance is not easy and it is not popular. As a result of their passion and commitment to change, feminists are accused of being angry. They want to change a system that does not work well for many of its members, but the system resists change. Feminist theologians care deeply about the welfare of women and men and the larger society in which they live. They want to see the world become a more whole and healthy place, not for selfish reasons or personal gain, but because they believe that the heart of the gospel is justice and peace for all God's people.

CHAPTER 2

Feminist Perspectives on the Bible

Imagine a conversation between three students that occurs the first day of a course in Christian Feminism. Susan says she attends a Bible-believing church. "I've been taught that the Bible is God's word and everything in it is true. The man was created first and the woman sinned first, so it is clear that men are meant to lead and women are meant to be submissive wives and mothers. The Bible does not allow women to be leaders of the church."

Barbara introduces herself as a women's studies major and says, "I think that the Bible has caused most of the problems women have in our society. It blames women for causing sin in the world. It treats women like property, not persons. It does not allow women positions of power and influence. The Bible was obviously written by men, about men, to promote a male agenda. It is not a good book for women."

Jenny says, "I grew up in the Presbyterian Church, and I've always considered myself both a Christian and a feminist. I am beginning to wonder if that is possible. If it is, what do Christian feminists do with the Bible?"

How can the same book provoke such different interpretations? Some readers think that the Bible imprisons women and restricts the options they have for their lives. Others conclude that the Bible empowers women to resist oppression and ultimately sets them free. The Bible is a symbol and a source of oppression for some women and a positive resource for others. This chapter will explore the underlying assumptions of these interpretations of the Bible and describe some of the ways that Christian feminists understand the Bible.

The Bible Is the Word of God

Some Christians believe that the Bible is literally a collection of God's words. A painting by Caravaggio shows Matthew sitting at a desk writing the Gospel that bears his name. A dove sits on Matthew's shoulder and whispers into his ear, an image implying that God dictated the words Matthew put to paper. The painting represents a perspective that considers the Bible inerrant or infallible, without error or fault. God's words are expressed clearly and truthfully in Scripture because although God used human stenographers, God did not permit human error or opinion to creep into the Bible.

If the Bible is God's Word, some Christians conclude, then it clearly expresses God's intentions for human beings. This belief is summarized by a bumper sticker I saw recently that proclaimed: "The Word of God Is the Will of God." The Bible provides true, trustworthy, and absolute answers to contemporary questions. It tells Christians what to believe and how to act. If the Bible says that wives should submit to their husbands and slaves to their masters, Christians should accept this as God's will for human relationships in the twentieth century as well as in the first. If the author of 1 Timothy will not permit a woman to teach or exercise authority, he is expressing God's intent for the contemporary church as well as for his own. The Bible is God's rule book for all times and places.

Many Christians believe that if the Bible is the Word and will of God, they must obey the whole Bible, even if it is difficult to understand or seems to contradict common sense. The Bible is part of God's mysterious plan for human lives, and humans have only a limited understanding of it. If the Bible challenges women to live out roles they do not like, such as submission to men, the problem is their lack of obedience, not the Bible's error or sexism. The Bible was not designed to make people feel good or to affirm their desire for power, equality, and justice. The Bible values self-sacrifice, not self-actualization. The Bible must be obeyed without question or debate because it is God's book and these are God's rules. Any ambiguity or softening of the rules implies a lack of respect for God's Word and God's will. The Bible is something like the instruction book for a chemistry lab. Students must follow the directions to the letter or risk blowing up the room.

A Christian who believes that the Bible is the inerrant Word of God might interpret its teachings about women as follows:

The creation story in Genesis 2–3 says that man was created first to be the leader and woman was created second to be his helpmate. Eve brought sin into the world because she spoke with the serpent, ate the forbidden fruit, and gave some to Adam. God punished Eve by giving men perpetual dominance over women and by giving women pain in childbirth. In the Old Testament the role of women was generally confined to being a wife and mother. A few exceptional women held leadership positions, but women were not permitted to serve in the priesthood.

In the New Testament Jesus did not include women among the twelve disciples, and he never ordained women to ministry. He treated women well, but did not challenge their subordinate social roles. When the church began to take shape, women did not serve as apostles, as did Paul and Peter. In fact, women were explicitly told to keep silent in the church (1 Cor 14:34) and were not permitted to teach or to have authority because Adam was formed first and Eve sinned first (1 Tim 2:12-14). Married women were told to submit to their husbands, just as slaves did to their masters and children to their parents (Eph 5:22-33).

Christians who believe that the Bible is the Word of God insist that these roles and instructions for women are still binding today. They might permit women to work outside the home and recognize the authority of women in business and government, but they do not accept women's leadership in the church.

Christians who think this way are deeply committed to Scripture and to the search for God's will. They do not shy away from the difficult or the uncomfortable, but are willing to be challenged by Scripture. They recognize the mystery of God and the limits of human understanding.

The literal approach to Scripture has its weaknesses, however. If everything in Scripture is absolutely true, then the Bible contains some inconsistencies. The apostle Paul wrote in 1 Corinthians 14 that women should keep silent in the church; but a few pages earlier, in 1 Corinthians 11, he said that when women prophesied in the church they should cover their heads. When he wrote to the Galatians, Paul insisted that there is no longer Jew nor Greek, slave nor free, male and female because all are one in Christ. Which of these words is truly the will of God?

If everything in the Bible is God's Word, readers might wonder about God's character. In Psalm 137 a frustrated author prayed for God to send an avenger who would take the children of his nation's enemies and dash their heads against a rock. When the Israelites became a nation, God frequently commanded them to destroy or enslave their political and religious enemies. If the Word of God is the will of God, do these social practices still reflect God's intentions for the world?

Even Christians who affirm the Bible as the Word of God do not consider every verse of the Bible equally applicable to their lives. They do not see every word as God's will for today. They claim they are not required to obey the dietary and sacrificial laws in Leviticus because Jesus abrogated them. They also recognize that some first-century cultural patterns are reflected in the Bible. The author of 1 Timothy, for example, instructed women to dress modestly and to avoid the gold and pearls that wealthy women wore. Men were told to raise their hands when they prayed. Many "Bible-believing" Christians do not enforce these rules, yet they insist that the verse that follows (forbidding women to teach or to have authority) is completely valid and is not a cultural issue (1 Tim 2:9-15). The criteria for making such a determination are somewhat unclear.

The Bible Is NOT the Word of God

Many feminists find such an interpretation of the Bible extremely disturbing. Read in this way, the Bible seems to be the source of women's contemporary troubles. It is no surprise that women are seen as sexual objects unfit for the workplace and leadership when the Bible considers them the source of evil and tells them they belong at home. Why should women believe in or obey a book that has so little regard for them? The Bible is an ancient book with no more authority than any other old book. It might offer some insight, but it is not a source of rules for contemporary living. The Bible is not the Word of God, but human words or, more precisely, male words. It was written in a patriarchal culture by men, for men, to men, and it is not good news for women. It is a dangerous book; it treats women badly; and it is not trustworthy, relevant, or authoritative for the present.

A feminist interpretation of biblical texts about women concludes that there is little in the Bible that is positive for women, and much that has been destructive. Women were regarded as little more than property. The tenth commandment told men not to covet a neighbor's wife, as if she were a possession like a servant, a house, or a donkey. Women rarely led independent lives, but were identified by their relationships, first as a daughter to a father, then as a wife to a husband. If a woman was raped, the violation was not against her, but against the man to whom she belonged, because rape diminished the value of a man's property. Women's primary purpose in life was to produce and rear children, so women's names, rights, and wishes were not considered very important.

When women do appear in nonmaternal roles, they are rarely praised or affirmed. Jezebel possessed some power and authority, but was portrayed as a wicked queen who threatened the religious life of the

Israelites (1 Kings 18; 19; 20). Gomer was the unfaithful wife of the prophet Hosea, and her actions provided a metaphor for the failures of the nation of Israel (Hosea 1). A woman appeared in the book of Proverbs, but she was a dangerous temptress who must be avoided (Proverbs 7). Michal criticized her husband David's outrageous behavior and was punished with childlessness (2 Sam 6:12-23). Rahab was a courageous foreign women who protected two Israelite spies; but when the author of the book of Hebrews praised her faith, he also felt compelled to remind readers that she was a prostitute (Joshua 2; Heb 11:31).

Feminists have noted the recurring issue for women in the Bible of their ritual uncleanness during the time of their menstrual periods and for seven days afterward (Lev 15:19-30). Touching an unclean woman or sitting in her chair rendered a man ritually unclean and temporarily unable to participate in religious ceremonies. Because of their uncleanness, women could not serve as priests in the temple or fully participate in worship and rituals. Feminists wonder why women are labeled unclean and denied access to religious life for something that is a natural part of life.

The Bible also records a number of incidents of violence against women. Hagar, the Egyptian maid, was forced to bear a child for her master Abraham and was then forced out into the wilderness when his wife, Sarah, became jealous of her (Gen 16:21). Tamar was raped by her half-brother (2 Sam 13:1-22). A woman was thrown outside to a group of men who raped her all night and left her dead, and her husband cared more about the violation of his property than about her death (Judges 19). Particularly troubling is the fact that this violence seems to be taken in stride. No one, especially God, seems to be very upset by these stories, which Phyllis Trible calls *Texts of Terror*. One of my students wrote after reading Judges 19, "I didn't even know what to think after it. To me it seemed like there should have been a big 'And the Lord was displeased' on the end of that story."

The New Testament demonstrates a kinder and gentler attitude toward women, but they still functioned in supporting roles. When they did something important, such as witness the resurrection, nobody believed them (Luke 24:1-11). When they demonstrated profound spiritual insight, it was forgotten (Mark 14:3-9). The Bible frequently commands women to be silent and submissive, reinforcing their secondary status. The Bible never challenges the persistent patriarchy and sexism reflected in it, but seems content with the status quo for women.

This feminist approach to the Bible takes seriously the patriarchy and sexism present there. The images of women as nameless, unclean baby machines are not the only images of women in Scripture, but they are very common, and readers need to think critically about their implications. Every year when I assign these texts to my students, several of them are shocked that such stories appear in the Bible. Sunday school lessons never mentioned rape and murder. These stories about women challenge their view of the Bible as a good book of moral lessons. Only when they look honestly at Scripture can they begin to consider what sort of book it is. Feminists ask appropriately whether women can give the Bible authority in their lives when its portrayal of women is so limited and destructive.

This critical approach to Scripture also recognizes its power to shape culture. Patriarchy may not have originated in the Bible, but it is certainly present there. Many people who do not read the Bible still believe that women are the source of evil, unclean, and subordinate to men. The assumptions in Scripture have influenced the beliefs of people who do not consider themselves Christian.

The feminist perspective on the Bible has its limitations. At times feminists seem to ask that the Bible meet twentieth-century Western standards of equality and justice without fully exploring the ways in which Scripture interacted with its ancient Near Eastern culture. Feminists have focused on the most violent and oppressive stories in the Bible, but pay less attention to the stories that challenged cultural norms in profoundly liberating ways. The feminist critique has also alienated some people because it has dismissed the Bible as an ancient patriarchal text without considering the reasons for its persistent influence. If the Bible is simply a collection of men's words, why didn't it lose its influence long ago? Many Christians believe Scripture speaks meaningfully because it is God's way of communicating, and they find it difficult to hear the critique of feminists who have no patience with the Bible.

The Christian Feminist Dilemma

The preceding discussion indicates that conservative Christians and secular feminists both conclude that the Bible advocates narrow and restrictive roles for women. The most conservative Christians then tell women to obey the Bible, while secular feminists advise women to reject it. It seems that women must accept and obey the whole Bible, like the bumper sticker that says, "God said it, I believe it, that settles it," or women must reject Scripture as hopelessly patriarchal.

Many Christian feminists believe that they are not limited to these two options, but can value both the Bible and feminism. A group of women from the Third World claimed that the Bible was a catalyst in their quest for human rights. "The Bible plays a vital role in the lives of women and

40

in our struggle for liberation, because the Bible itself is a book about life and liberation. . . . The Gospels restore to women our human dignity as persons loved and cherished by God."[1] Rigoberta Menchu, a Guatemalan Indian who won the Nobel Peace Prize, wrote of the struggle for economic equity, "For us the Bible is our main weapon. It has shown us the way. . . . When we started using the Bible, when we began studying it in terms of our reality, it was because we found in it a document to guide us." Menchu had been taught that the Bible told the poor to accept their poverty, but when she read it she found that the Bible encouraged the struggle against injustice.[2] Chung Hyun Kyung described the experience of a Filipino woman who read the Bible and discovered that marriage was about equality, not obedience. "This we have learned from Bible study—freedom and equal rights."[3] Cheryl Sanders wrote, "The Bible has been a significant source of spiritual, ethical, and political empowerment for black women. . . . It has supplied the chief rationale for their resistance to human suffering and oppression, mandated their moral teachings and practice, and resourced their affirmations of racial, cultural, and sexual identity."[4] Renita Weems wrote, "African American women have continued to read the Bible in most instances because of its vision and promise of a world where the humanity of everyone will be fully valued."[5]

The Bible provides a rationale for resistance? The Bible restores dignity to women? The Bible teaches freedom and equal rights? Are these Christian feminists reading the same Bible discussed above? Perhaps reading the Bible is more complex than bumper sticker proclamations suggest.

If feminist theologians can find encouragement and positive role models in the Bible, perhaps they are reading it differently than either secular feminists or conservative Christians. Both of these groups tend to read it literally, rather than critically. They neglect many of the positive passages about women and fail to consider the cultural and literary contexts of the negative passages.

Feminist biblical scholars have found and brought to life many hidden or neglected stories of women in the Bible. There were women who took courageous and wise action, challenged the status quo, and were not primarily defined by their children. Miriam watched over her infant brother Moses when he was floating in the Nile and later led the Israelites through the wilderness along with Moses and Aaron (Exodus 2; Numbers 12). Vashti was a queen who refused to degrade herself by displaying her beauty before the king's friends (Esther 1). Jael offered hospitality to, then killed the leader of an enemy army (Judges 4). Priscilla was a leader and a teacher in the early church (Rom 16:2-4).

41

Elisabeth Schüssler Fiorenza argued that the women who are mentioned in the Bible represent only the tip of the iceberg. Using her knowledge of biblical and extrabiblical evidence about the role of women in the first century, she approached Scripture with the assumption that if Paul spoke to a group of people about spiritual gifts, he meant both men and women. If the biblical texts identified a few women as leaders of house churches, there were probably others as well. If the first-century writers made a point of prohibiting women from preaching and leadership, they were most likely already active in these roles. Schüssler Fiorenza believes that readers need to look beneath the surface of the Bible.

Other feminist biblical scholars explore the stories of women in a variety of ways. *Searching the Scriptures: A Feminist Introduction* includes a number of essays in which scholars describe the principles they or others use to interpret Scripture. The *Women's Bible Commentary* contains analyses of the books of the Bible with an emphasis on the role and treatment of women. Many other recent books examine neglected stories of women in the Bible. A particularly imaginative approach can be found in Miriam Therese Winter's books, *The Gospel According to Mary*, and *The Chronicles of Noah and Her Sisters*. Winter wondered how it might be different if women were telling the story of Jesus or the early days of the Israelites and then rewrote these stories through the eyes of women.

Some feminists consider it pointless to describe a few token women in the midst of overwhelming masculinity and patriarchy. Such activity seems to play games with an androcentric text. If the stories of women must be teased out like a diamond from the rough, or if the role of women has to be imagined, the Bible appears to be hopeless. In 1973 Phyllis Trible proposed that the Bible could be depatriarchalized if readers were able to discard the patriarchal lenses that shaped their reading. If readers simply saw Scripture on its own terms without assuming, for example, that women were the source of evil, they would find that the Bible did not support male domination as much as men claimed. In response, Mary Daly wondered about the length of such a depatriarchalized Bible. Perhaps, she suggested, there would be enough for an interesting pamphlet.[6]

The strategy of accentuating positive texts and de-emphasizing negative ones can lead to a kind of scoreboard contest over which side accumulates more evidence. If feminists can find enough positive stories about women to outweigh the negative, does that mean the Bible can still be believed? How should readers weigh the Bible's frequent silence about women? This raises the broader and essential question of how we are to approach, read, and interpret the Bible. Over the last two centuries biblical scholarship has emphasized the need to read the text in light of the historical and cultural contexts in which it was written. Three questions can help guide the reading of the Bible: (1) What kind of book is this? (2) Why should anyone believe it? (3) What principles or interpretive strategies should be used?

What Kind of Book Is This? God's Word, Human Words

The Bible is a long book written over a span of about two thousand years and completed almost two thousand years ago. Several dozen authors from very different times and places contributed to the Bible. It deals with many different topics, cultural situations, and environments, from the height of Israel's power to Israel's exile in Babylon.

Many biblical scholars suggest that the Bible is not the Word of God in an absolute, literal sense. God did not dictate the Bible to a secretary or make an audiotape of the essential teachings, which a typist transcribed verbatim. There is enough ambiguity, repetition, and disagreement that it is difficult to see the Bible as God's crystal clear mandate to humanity. Rather, the Bible is composed of human words written in response to God's actions. Sandra Schneiders wrote: "The Bible is literally the word of human beings about their experience of God."[7] Human beings encountered God and found the relationship so compelling and life changing that they continued to speak and write about it.

This makes the Bible more of a storybook than a rule book. It is a narrative about God rather than a recording of God's actual words. Not every word reflects the will of God because the words have been filtered through human brains, lives, and pens and inevitably reflect the assumptions, attitudes, and behavior patterns of the culture. Human understanding is imperfect, as is the ability to articulate something so mysterious as the encounter with God. This implies that the biblical authors could not anticipate the historical circumstances of the twentieth century, and therefore their words are not always applicable now. It also implies that the biblical writings cannot be required to meet twentieth-century standards of justice, equity, and church life in order for them to say something valid and meaningful. The Bible simply does not answer many contemporary questions.

If the Bible is a human book, subject to human frailty and cultural context, what distinguishes it from other books and accounts for its power and influence? The Bible continues to speak because it captures some of the timeless, recurring issues of humanity—pain, passion, power, greed, loss, despair, and disease. It describes a caring God who acted in the past and suggests that this God is present to contemporary readers as well. The experiences of people who encountered God in the past give insight to those who meet God now. The Bible also speaks the painful truth about the human condition—that we often damage each other and ourselves. That is not God's will, but the reason for redemption.

The Bible continues to speak, some scholars believe, because Scripture is more than a human book. It can transcend the limitations of its authors because God chose to use human words and experiences to communicate divine truth.[8] God accommodated to human capacity and spoke, as it were, with a lisp or a stammer, so that God's Word in Scripture could be understood by human beings. When patriarchy and slavery appear in Scripture, they are part of God's accommodation to human capacity, not God's intentions for eternity.[9] Letty Russell observed that it is dangerous to call the Bible the Word of God if by that one means that everything in it reflects God's intention or will for the world. "But divine inspiration means that God's Spirit has the power to make the story speak to us from faith to faith. The Bible is accepted as the Word of God when communities of faith understand God to be speaking to them in and through its message."[10]

The Bible will not always be easy to hear. It makes difficult demands. It asks readers to care for the poor, to put another's interests ahead of their own, to give up personal desires for the good of the community. It calls readers to new ways of living that are not always comfortable. Readers, like the biblical writers, are limited by their humanity and sinfulness and will not understand or like everything they read. Johanna Bos wrote: "If the Bible is the living Word of God, it might be as surprising and unmanageable as God."[11] The Bible cannot be domesticated. It has the power to both shock and transform all its readers, even feminists.

Why Believe It? The Authority of the Bible

The Bible often serves as the center of Christian worship and sermons. What gives it credibility and relevance? Why do people give it power to shape their lives? What is the nature of its authority?[12]

Some people grant the Bible authority because they see it as a divine rule book descended from heaven to tell people what to do. It is God's Word and must be obeyed without question. Any challenge to any part of the Bible threatens to undercut its credibility and influence. If the apostle Paul did not write the books of Ephesians or 1 Timothy, as the books say, the validity of the entire Bible is compromised. Recognizing the authority of the Bible means accepting every word as God's Word and will.

Other people do not believe that the Bible has any claim on their lives. There are Christians who listen to the reading of Scripture on Sunday morning and do not reject it outright, but they know so little about its content that it has no real function in their lives. Some feminists insist that the Bible has no authority because it is an ancient book with many outdated and offensive ideas and therefore need not be granted any influence in their lives.

It is also possible to understand Scripture as a document that says something true and meaningful about the human condition and therefore invites assent, as when Claudia Camp described authority as "a free surrendering to the jurisdiction of Scripture."[13] In this understanding of authority, people try to live according to the Bible's principles, not because God coerces or threatens them, but because Scripture at its best gives meaning, purpose, and guidance. They choose to say yes to the Bible because they believe it has something valuable to say to them.

Feminist theologians speak in many ways about the importance of Scripture in their lives. Renita Weems wrote, "Where the Bible has been able to capture the imagination of African American women, it has been and continues to be able to do so because significant portions speak to the deepest aspirations of oppressed people for freedom, dignity, justice, and vindication."[14] Ada Maria Isasi-Diaz explained that for Hispanic women the Bible is meaningful, not because it is the Word of God, but because its stories provide insight and courage. "Bible stories become *ours* when we use them because we need them."[15] Letty Russell described her encounter with Scripture:

> The Bible has authority in my life because it makes sense of my experience and speaks to me about the meaning and purpose of my humanity in Jesus Christ. In spite of its ancient and patriarchal worldviews, in spite of its inconsistencies and mixed messages, the story of God's love affair with the world leads me to a vision of New Creation that impels my life. . . . For me the Bible is "scripture," or sacred writing, because it functions as "script," or prompting for life.[16]

One text that provides such prompting for life is Mark 5, where two stories are woven together. Jairus came to Jesus seeking healing for his twelve-year-old daughter, and Jesus agreed to go to his home. On the way, Jesus encountered a woman who had suffered from a bleeding disease for twelve years, which made her ritually unclean and an outcast from synagogue and society. Jesus was surrounded by a crowd, so the woman was able to approach him without being noticed and touch his clothes. She was immediately healed, and Jesus felt power go out of him. When he asked who had touched him, the woman told him what had happened to her, and Jesus affirmed her deep faith and promised her healing and wholeness. A messenger came to tell Jairus that his daughter had died, but Jesus went on to the house and raised the girl from the dead. Women who read this story encounter Jesus, who values women even though they were not high priorities in his culture. Jesus was not bound by laws about ritual purity or social interaction with women. He affirmed the woman's faith and encouraged Jairus to have the same faith she did. Jesus gave freedom and dignity to the woman and new life to the child, and his treatment of women provides hope for contemporary readers who seek healing and dignity.

How to Read It? Principles of Interpretation

How do we read the Bible? If it is influenced by the culture, opinions, and experiences of the author, and if the authors sometimes contradict each other and themselves, is it possible to make any sense of it at all? How does the reader discern what the text meant when it was written and what it might mean now? This is particularly important when reading the texts that most restrict women.

The texts that have historically had the most power to portray women negatively or to restrict their roles are the stories of the creation and fall in Genesis 1–3 and Paul's instructions that women should submit to their husbands, be silent in the church, and refrain from teaching or exercising authority over men. Gerda Lerner observed, "These biblical core texts sat like huge boulders across the paths women had to travel in order to define themselves as equals of men."[17] In other texts Paul was quite positive about women, assuming their presence, leadership, and gifts; but the references were more subtle. The negative passages, 1 Timothy 2, 1 Corinthians 11 and 14, and Ephesians 5, are very explicit and are often presented as the Pauline position without reference to the texts where he speaks of women as his coworkers or as church leaders.

As readers try to understand what the text said and meant to its hearers in the first century, and what it means to contemporary readers, they might ask four questions.

What is the historical context?

The Bible arose out of a patriarchal culture in which men ruled and were the center of life. Its authors found nothing unusual in the role of women as nameless daughters and wives who belonged to their fathers and husbands. The fact that the Bible reflects those patriarchal assumptions does not mean that patriarchy is God's will, but rather that the authors could not escape their cultural contexts. In the story of Hagar, Sarah, and Abraham, for example, the use of a slave women as a surrogate mother was not unusual in a culture that valued women for their ability to bear children. If a woman's entire identity depended on producing children, she would take desperate measures to ensure that she had them. God did not approve of the practice or suggest it should be valid for all time. On the contrary, the text illustrates the competition, jealousy, and destructiveness that resulted.

When the author of 1 Timothy told women that they could not teach or have authority, he did so out of a culture where women were seldom educated or respected as leaders. He may have known of women involved in forms of Christianity he considered heretical and therefore tried to protect the community from the influence of false teaching. Readers can sympathize with his intentions without agreeing that his advice is similarly valid for the twentieth century.

Understanding the historical context is particularly essential when Scripture offers a radical challenge to the surrounding culture. The book of Ruth is remarkable because a young woman chose to be linked, not to a man who could protect her, but to her mother-in-law, who had no money, position, or authority. This is a story about the loyalty of two women to each other and the initiative and effort they put into their survival. When the reader can see the odds against them, the story becomes an even more powerful example of women's strength and courage.

What is the literary context?

How does a particular text or set of verses fit into the larger document? How does the context help to explain the meaning of a specific text? The verses in which Paul commands women to keep silent in the church (1 Cor 14:34-35) are embedded in a lengthy passage about appropriate worship and use of spiritual gifts. Paul wanted worship to be carried out in a decent and orderly way. He did not want people showing off their spiritual gifts or speaking out of turn. Some commentators suggest that the women in Corinth were interrupting the services to ask questions and that this verse reflects Paul's desire for decorum. Feminist biblical scholars observe that, although this may have been a legitimate and appropriate request for first-century Corinth, it is not necessarily God's will for women in the twentieth century.

Another difficult text is Ephesians 5:22-33, which begins, "Wives, be subject to your husbands as you are to the Lord. For the husband is the head of the wife just as Christ is the head of the church." Ephesians 5:21

47

("Be subject to one another out of reverence for Christ") is not always bundled with these verses, but it should be because it sets a context of mutual submission that shapes the interpretation of the following verses about marriage. It is also important to note that Ephesians 6:5-9 instructs slaves to obey their earthly masters. Even the most conservative biblical interpreters do not suggest that slavery is currently the will of God.

Literary context is also important for interpreting the story about the concubine in Judges 19. The story lacks a clear statement that God was displeased, as my student correctly noted; but the entire book of Judges is an indictment of the sins of the Israelites, who were completely out of control and lacking in basic human decency. The story of the concubine can be seen as a particularly gruesome illustration of the behavior that occurs when people lack a sense of God's presence in their lives. The book of Judges as a whole reports that God was deeply displeased with the way people treated one another.

What is the author's purpose or intention?

Why did the author write a particular book or text? The New Testament letters were written to specific congregations or groups of people and often addressed questions or issues that had occurred in that community. The psalms, on the other hand, are honest expressions of human doubt, conflict, and faith. They articulate the deepest emotions of people struggling to encounter God and make sense of the world. When the psalmist asks God to destroy the babies of his enemies, he expresses, not the will of God, but, rather, a common human desire for vengeance.

When reading the Bible, then, we need to ask whether the author is defining the essence of the gospel or responding to a specific issue in the experience of the readers. Is the author suggesting a solution to a particular problem or making an absolute rule? In 1 Corinthians, for example, Paul did not show a very high regard for marriage. He encouraged the Corinthian Christians to remain single if they could, although he conceded that marriage was permitted to those who lacked self-control. His purpose, however, was not to insist that marriage and sexuality were bad for Christians, nor to deny them the pleasures of the body. He believed that Jesus would return to earth in the next few years and that while they waited Christians should spend all their energy proclaiming the gospel. Spouses and families would divert them from their work.

Authorial intention is also an important factor in the interpretation of the purity laws embedded in the book of Leviticus. The book contains numerous laws about sacrifices, worship, social relationships, health, diet, and sexuality. These laws are not established simply for their own sake, but as a sign of holiness and purity. The Israelites were to be a distinct people, clearly different and separate from the nations around them. The laws served as boundaries that helped to define the Israelites and distance them from their neighbors. The body of the individual seemed to serve as a symbol of the larger community. The deep concern about dirt and purity, about what entered and exited the individual body, seemed very much connected to the purity of the nation. This does not fully resolve the problem of the purity laws for women, but it does help to set them in a larger context of concern for everyone's purity.[18]

How does the text fit into the whole biblical story?

This question is particularly important when the Bible seems to contradict itself, as it does on the issues of slavery and women. The Israelites held slaves and were commanded only to treat them well, not to free them. Slavery was also common in the first century, and both slaves and owners joined the Christian community. As Christians began to understand the implications of the gospel, they realized that enslaving other humans was not compatible with the Christian faith. They also recognized that social institutions could not be transformed immediately. Paul believed that in Christ there is no distinction between slave and free (Gal 3:28), but he also told a slave to return to his master (Philemon) and urged slaves to obey their masters (Eph 6:5-9). Such ambiguity does not mean Paul suffered from multiple personality disorder, but that he was caught between his deep commitment to the gospel and the awareness that social structures change slowly. His tolerance of slavery did not mean that slavery was or is anything other than a sign of sinfulness, but fully living out the gospel is a process that takes time and is still not complete in the present.

Scripture demonstrates a similar ambiguity about the role of women. Paul wrote in Galatians 3:28 that in Christ there are no distinctions between male and female. He recognized the leadership of Prisca, Phoebe, Junia, Euodia, and Syntyche in the early church (Rom 16:1-7; Phil 4:2-3). Paul's letters report that women prophesied and evangelized, led house churches, and instructed both male and female Christians. Women in the early church found freedom to lead, to speak, and to use their spiritual gifts; but this freedom clashed with social realities because women who took public roles in religious ceremonies could be mistaken for temple prostitutes. The disregard for gender differences and social status in Christian congregations threatened the hierarchical Greco-Roman culture. Paul did not want the Christian faith to needlessly offend outsiders or to invite more persecution, so he advised particular congregations that women (and at times men) should be cautious with their new freedom. Elisabeth Schüssler Fiorenza argued that as the

49

churches developed they became even more cautious and conservative as their conflicts with surrounding cultures increased. The letter to Timothy may have been written more than fifty years after Paul's letter to the Galatians, which would account for some of the discrepancy.[19]

Rita Nakashima Brock wrote of this ambiguity in Paul, "Rather than trying to decide whether he was sexist or liberating in his attitudes toward women, it may be more honest to say he was both, as he was by turns egalitarian and authoritarian."[20] Paul believed that the gospel breaks down the barriers between Jew and Greek, slave and free, male and female. He saw how effectively some women exercised leadership in the church, but his understanding of the gospel conflicted with his education and assumptions, which did not recognize women as capable of authority or learning. Like the rest of us, Paul was not always consistent. He was a human being, wrestling with issues and trying to make sense of the Christian faith for people of his time. One of the most crucial questions for twentieth-century readers is to discern how Scripture continues to speak to them in their own time and place.

How do we decide? Criteria for evaluating texts

How do fallible people presume to determine which parts of the Bible should shape their lives and which arose out of the cultural situation of their authors and were not meant to define contemporary life and behavior? Critics charge that this gives readers power to pick and choose what to believe, because anything offensive can be automatically labeled an ancient cultural issue and therefore considered irrelevant.

Evaluating texts does not mean determining their worth or truth. Exodus 35–40 contains elaborate details for sewing clothes for priests and constructing the tabernacle where the Israelites worshiped in the wilderness. The texts are true and valid in that they provided instructions for the orderly worship of God. Most contemporary Christians do not believe God requires them to worship in tabernacles or offer animal sacrifices, but they might still learn from the passage in Exodus that worship space is holy, that care ought to be exercised in creating it, and that God ought to be approached with a sense of awe.

Scripture itself suggests that some parts of the tradition are more definitive than others. Judaism emphasized obedience to the law as an important means of relating to God, but Jesus redefined both the obedience and the relationship. He appeared to make the law even more demanding when he said in the Sermon on the Mount, "You have heard that it was said, 'You shall love your neighbor and hate your enemy.' But I say to you, Love your enemies and pray for those who persecute you" (Matt 5:43-44). Similarly, he made the laws about anger, adultery, and retaliation almost impossible to keep, but that was his point. The law is not the primary basis of a relationship with God. Paul wrote to the Galatians that although the law was essential for Judaism, Christians no longer live under its requirements. Jesus and Paul contradicted the Old Testament even though they valued it as God's word. They established a new set of criteria, which made faith and grace the center of Christianity.

For Paul, the timeless or central truth of the gospel was justification by grace through faith. People are made right with God not because of what they do but because of what God has done for them. Scholars call this approach the "canon within the canon," which means that within the accepted canon, or list of writings finally gathered into the Bible, there is a subset of texts that serve as the central theme by which all others must be measured. Martin Luther agreed with Paul that the central theme of the gospel is justification by grace through faith, which led him to question the inclusion in the canon of the book of James. Luther called it an "epistle of straw" because it places so much emphasis on good works.

Discerning a central theme requires the reader to make judgments about which parts of the Bible constitute its essential message and which parts represent culturally conditioned advice. Scripture assists with this process by highlighting these central themes. Teresa Okure argued that the liberating elements of the Bible, such as the equality of men and women, the creation of women in God's image, and Jesus' affirmation of women, came from God and thus represent the timeless truths of salvation. The oppressive elements, such as the inferiority and sinfulness of women, the command of submission, and the rules about purity, arose out of a human and culturally conditioned perspective.[21] Okure believed that Paul articulated the essence of the gospel in Galatians 3:28, but reflected the limits of his humanity and culture when he instructed wives and slaves to submit to their husbands and masters.

Defining a central theme enabled some feminist theologians to minimize the impact of the negative passages. Elsa Tamez criticized feminists who dismiss the Bible without understanding its central message.

> The tendency of some First World radical feminists to reject the Bible, is, it seems to me, an exaggerated reaction. I think that by assigning too much importance to these peripheral texts [Gen. 3], many leave aside the central message, which is profoundly liberating. From my point of view, it is precisely the gospel's spirit of justice and freedom that neutralizes antifemale texts....A time has come to acknowledge that those biblical texts that reflect patriarchal culture and proclaim women's inferiority and their submission to men are not normative; neither are those texts that legitimize slavery normative.[22]

Rosemary Ruether suggested that a central theme in Scripture is the prophetic principle. The prophets and Jesus frequently criticized hierarchy, legalism, and the abuse of power and wealth and recognized that even the best religious impulses could be corrupted by greed, power, and privilege. When the Israelites achieved political power they failed to care for the poor and outcast; the prophets reminded the people of the need to do justice, but the prophets failed to recognize the deep-seated patriarchy in the tradition. The assumptions of their culture made them blind to their own failings. Feminist theology, Ruether argued, has continued the prophetic principle by applying it to the problem of sexism.[23]

Another central theme often used to evaluate biblical texts is the character of God. Would a merciful and just God, who encourages people to treat each other well and care for the poor, encourage sexist or racist behavior? Sandra Schneiders asked bluntly, "In what sense can one regard as word of God that which, in some respects at least, cannot possibly be attributed to God without rendering God the enemy and the oppressor of some human beings?"[24] Elsa Tamez pointed out that even readers who are not biblical scholars automatically deal with the sexist texts by saying that "reality should be different today, that God is a God of life, and therefore he cannot favor discrimination against women."[25] Letty Russell wrote, "For my part, I cannot imagine a God who does not seek to be a partner with all humankind in the mending of creation."[26] Teresa Okure wrote, "In whatever way we look at it, no oppressive element in the Bible can be attributed to God's will. God is by nature the liberator of the oppressed; God cannot ipso facto be an oppressor in any form of the word."[27] Renita Weems noted that the biblical texts that speak of justice and liberation present "a portrait of a God that oppressed readers can believe in."[28]

There are other readers of the biblical tert, however, who identify God's judgment as the central theme in Scripture. They argue that God sets rules and expects people to live by them. Obedience is more essential than justice for the oppressed. Maintaining the status quo is more biblical than turning social institutions upside down. Since people choose different central themes, obviously the canon within the canon approach does not guarantee that Scripture will be interpreted in a liberating way. Some feminist theologians argue that because Scripture fails to unequivocally support the equality of women, it cannot provide the norms or criteria for its own interpretation. The criterion for evaluating Scripture, Elisabeth Schüssler Fiorenza argued, is not the book itself, but the experience of women.[29] What in the Bible is good and helpful for women? Ada Maria Isasi-Diaz illustrated this approach when she wrote, "Hispanic women's experience and our struggle for survival, not the

Bible, are the source of our theology and the starting point for how we should interpret, appropriate, and use the Bible." The Bible is authoritative "only insofar as it contributes to Hispanic women's struggle for liberation."[30]

Women's own sense of right and wrong helps them to make sense of Scripture. Renita Weems advised readers to "resist those things within the culture and the Bibe that one finds obnoxious or antagonistic to one's innate sense of identity and to one's basic instincts for survival."[31] Margaret Farley wrote that Scripture "cannot be believed unless it rings true to our deepest capacity for truth and goodness. If it contradicts this, it is not to be believed." Critics would ask if the Bible is "really required to answer the demands of reason and the cries of the human heart," but Farley replied that religious traditions have power only as they help to make sense of human life. Religious traditions do not have to be easy or completely rational, but they cannot do violence to our most basic convictions.[32] Equality and mutuality are two such convictions, and whatever violates them cannot be seen as authoritative.

Suspicion and Trust

Kathleen Norris, describing the process by which she integrated feminism and the Christian faith, said that she read the Bible "with a certain suspicion, with a wary eye on who is doing the telling, and who is left out, marginalized, or demeaned." She found this a useful way of reading, but she added, "I soon realized that reading with suspicion worked best when I also read with trust, with belief enough to nourish my developing faith."[33]

Interpreting the Bible is a complicated task that requires study, effort, humility, suspicion, and trust. There are many difficult passages in Scripture from which people claim divine justification for treating each other badly. There are ugly stories of human brokenness and failure. And yet there is also something liberating about Scripture, such as God's care for the poor, God's persistent love of resistant people, Jesus' relationships with women and other outcasts, and the counter cultural witness of the early church. God's passion and compassion shine through. God demonstrates deep care for the world and all its people, for women as well as men. God uses fallible human beings and their stammering voices to communicate profound truth about God's justice, care, and shalom. When all is said and done, God's good news has the last word. And it is good news for all.

CHAPTER 3

Language About God

When you think about God, what picture or image comes into your mind?

When Michelangelo painted the Creation on the ceiling of the Sistine Chapel, he portrayed God as a bearded, kindly, mature man reaching out with his fingers to a younger version of himself. Celie, in Alice Walker's *The Color Purple*, also described God as a bearded white man with blue-gray eyes. In the movie *The Ten Commandments* God was not visible, but possessed a deep male voice. A popular religious song asserts, "He's got the whole world in his hands." Many Christians pray to "Our Father, who art in heaven." In colloquial terms, God is "the man upstairs."

Many people envision God as a kind, gentle, elderly man who may resemble a beloved grandfather. We may think of God as the grumpy, but soft-hearted, Mr. Wilson in the "Dennis the Menace" comic strips. We may envision God as an absent father who cares about us, but is so busy working that he is never around. Or perhaps our first image of God is that of a stern and unforgiving judge. Many, perhaps even most, of the assumptions and images we have of God are of a male figure.

If pressed, many of us would quickly insist that God is not really a male. God transcends sexuality. God is not defined by gender as humans are. He is a Spirit. But then, why do we so often call God *he*? Some people appeal to Scripture and tradition to reply that "The Bible calls God *he*. Jesus refers to God as *he* and *Father*. These names and pronouns are always used in worship. This is what I have always been taught."

Some people appeal to the rules of language or grammar. "*He* includes *he* and *she*. It is a generic term. When we use it, we don't really mean God is male; but we must have a personal pronoun to speak of God, and *he* is more inclusive than *she*."

Others defend the use of male language for God by citing the relative value of male and female in our culture. "Calling God *she* would insult him! God *certainly* isn't a WOMAN!"

Others dismiss the entire topic as completely irrelevant, unimportant, and uninteresting. "Why are we talking about this issue? It doesn't matter what we call God. Why do feminists want to change everything?"

The Problem of God Language

A little girl wrote a letter to God in which she asked, "Dear God, are boys better than girls? I know you are one, but try to be fair."[1] A four-year-old daughter of feminist parents is convinced that God is a boy, despite her mother's use of feminine pronouns.

Feminist theologians believe that language about God matters a great deal because it reflects our deepest beliefs about God and ourselves. They want to change, or at least to expand, some of the language traditionally used for God because they believe it has contributed to an excessively narrow understanding of God.

A message board outside a church contained this quotation: "Those who are born of God are growing to resemble Him." Are women included in this? Can a woman resemble a man? Should she be asked to? "Well, of course," church members might reply, "women and men equally grow to resemble God in love, faith, hope, and justice." And yet the church belongs to a denomination that does not ordain women as ministers and elders. If God is a he, does men's greater resemblance to God give them the right of ordination?

A worship service in a Protestant or a Roman Catholic church illustrates the nature of the language commonly used for God. The opening hymn might be "Praise, My Soul, the King of Heaven," or "This Is My Father's World." The minister may begin the service with the phrase, "In the name of the Father, and the Son, and the Holy Spirit." The call to worship might include the phrase, "For he is our God, and we are the people of his pasture, and the sheep of his hand" (Ps 95:7). The assurance of forgiveness may include the words, "I am He who blots out your transgressions" (Isa 43:25). The Apostles' Creed begins, "I believe in God the Father Almighty." The Lord's Prayer begins, "Our Father, who art in heaven." The closing hymn might be "All Creatures of Our God and King," which in some older versions contains more than a dozen male pronouns for God in seven verses.

These examples suggest that even if we are more sophisticated than the little girls who think God is a boy, religious language is permeated with male imagery and pronouns. God may not actually be a man, but when we talk about God in worship and elsewhere our language describes exactly that—a man.

Feminist theologians argue that traditional language about God takes one dimension of the divine—God as Father—and elevates it to an exclusive position, refusing to allow other images that express something equally biblical and true about God. The emphasis on God as King, Lord, and Master means that we think of God as a powerful, controlling ruler. This is a valid biblical image, but the Bible images God in other ways that are often neglected.

Male language for God also implies that men are more like God or closer to God's image. If we see God as a man or more like a man or more properly named in male language, we tend to think of men as more like God, and women as less like God. Mary Daly captured the essence of this problem with her pithy phrase, "If God is male, then the male is God."[2]

Predominantly male language for God can make it difficult for some people to relate to God in a positive way. Women and men who have been physically, sexually, or emotionally abused by their fathers find it difficult to think of God primarily as a father. Even if one's father has been absent rather than abusive, the sense that daddy was never there may make it difficult to experience God the Father as a comforting presence in one's life.[3]

Finally, feminist theologians challenge the easy acceptance of dominantly male language for God. Why does this language seem so obvious? Why is it so difficult to change? Why is it so difficult to think critically about it?

The Persistence and Power of Masculine God Language

Feminist theologians have identified several reasons why the link between God and maleness persists despite the disclaimer that God is not "really" a man. The Bible, the history of Christianity, theological language, liturgy, education, and custom all contribute to the pervasiveness of male God language. The feminist critique attempts to describe the power of the tradition, the nature of its influence, and the difficulty of change.

One of the most common reasons for using male language for God is that the Bible uses male pronouns and titles for God. "God created humankind in his image, in the image of God he created them, male and female he created them" (Gen 1:27). A recurring theme in Israel's history contrasted the one God of the Israelites, who transcended sexuality but was still called he, and the multiple idols, fertility cults, and female deities of the surrounding nations. God is occasionally referred to as father to illustrate that the God of Abraham and Sarah, Rebekah and Isaac was powerfully and persistently related to the people. Jeremiah asserts that God is a father to Israel, a particularly hopeful and comforting image to people in exile who wondered if God had abandoned them (Jer 31:9).

In the Christian Scriptures Jesus often referred to God as his Father. Some Christians argue that if Jesus called God Father, they should also. Jesus brings us into a relationship with God, and his Father becomes our Father. If Jesus used it, it must be good, right, and appropriate. After all, Jesus never called God Mother![4]

As the Christian tradition developed over the next twenty centuries, theologians continued to use male pronouns for God. The language of creed, liturgy, and hymns was similarly masculine. God was powerful, awesome, and totally in control, as the Westminster Confession affirms:

> There is but one only living and true God, who is infinite in being and perfection, a most pure spirit, invisible, without body, parts, or passions, immutable, immense, eternal, incomprehensible, almighty, most wise, most holy, most free, most absolute, working all things according to the counsel of his own immutable and most righteous will, for his own glory.

Daphne Hampson observed that descriptions such as these suggest that God is all-powerful, complete in himself, and self-sufficient. "Is He, one wonders, the reflection of what have been many a man's wildest dreams?"[5] Such descriptions of God reflect the deep human desire for life to be orderly, sensible, and controlled. Only men have traditionally had this kind of power in the world.

Children are educated early into the tradition that describes God in male terms. In a church that prides itself on its inclusive language in worship, two-year-old children in Sunday school still learn from the teacher and the curriculum that God is he. After six years in a feminist household and a year of reading Bible stories aloud, my son asked why I always changed the he's to God, when after all, God is a he. My daughter, reared to pray "God is great, God is good, let us thank God for our food," suddenly began to hesitate when she prayed and soon was reluctant to pray at all. She had moved into a new room at her day care, and there the regular lunchtime prayer was phrased, "let us thank *Him* for our food. . . . "

When children who are educated this way become college students or adults, they cannot understand why anyone would question what is so incredibly obvious to them. Of course God is referred to with male pronouns. They have not been told of any alternatives and have rarely been asked to examine their assumptions.

A more subtle, but equally powerful, factor in our view of God is that many of us have been effectively socialized to believe that maleness and men are better or more important than femaleness and women. Men are stronger, wiser, smarter, and braver than women; and so God must be a man or at least more like a man or described in male language. Many people need to think of God in male terms because they do not think women or mothers are powerful enough to be in charge.

Women have often been portrayed in the Christian tradition not only as weaker than men, but also as far more sexual. Several critics of feminist theology have claimed that speaking of God in female or maternal terms introduces sexuality into the nature of God. Feminine sexuality and childbirth are seen as particularly demeaning to God.

> If God is addressed in female terms, however, his holy otherness is lost sight of. If God is called Mother, the metaphor system of birthing, suckling, carrying in the womb comes into play; and the divine Mother is then portrayed as giving birth to creation. . . . This is the ultimate idolatry, in which the Trinity is destroyed, the holy otherness of God from creation is lost, and human beings have usurped the place of their creator.[6]

The word *he* apparently transcends sexuality. At first this argument seems to transcend logic as well, but there are many English words in which the female version is inferior to the male or is sexualized in a particular way. A master is skillful or in charge; a mistress is an illicit sexual partner. A lord manages property; a lady has perfect manners and breeding, but does little more than drink tea. Sir is a term of respect; a madam runs a brothel. Christians throughout history have considered the female and the feminine at best subordinate, and at worst, dangerous. They did not think they honored God by calling God Mother or Midwife.

Even the limitations of English grammar contribute to the problem of God language. The Christian tradition values a personal God, and "it" seems too impersonal. Since English has no personal, gender-neutral pronoun (as do other languages), we must choose between a male or female personal pronoun. For centuries "he" has been considered generic, or true of both sexes, so it has been the pronoun of choice for the deity. This linguistic quirk enables people to repeatedly refer to God as he, even while claiming that God is not male or female.

Feminine language for God makes many people uncomfortable. References to God as she are disturbing because they are new and different, they feel unnatural, or they seem demeaning to God. In response to an article about God language in a denominational magazine, a man wrote a brief, but pointed, response: "If God the Father leaves my church, I'm going with him."

Given the powerful Christian tradition and the pointed feminist critique, it is not surprising that there are sharp conflicts over language about God. The publication of the *Inclusive Language Lectionary*, which substituted the "Reign of God" for the "Kingdom of God," "Sovereign" for "Lord," and added "[and Mother]" after the word Father, caused enormous controversy, including accusations that the authors were "castrating God."[7] The Christian Reformed Church recently decided that it was acceptable to say God was something like a mother, but not to address God as Mother. Worship services have been arenas for conflict when some members insist on retaining Father language for God and others ask that it be eliminated. These discussions are heated and not entirely rational because they evoke strong feelings about the nature of God and humanity.

Feminist theologians have not simply criticized the tradition, but have thoughtfully and creatively begun to revision it. Their contributions include reflection on the mystery of God, the meaning of metaphors, the use of maternal and other feminine images for God, and the need for many names to describe God.[8]

The Mystery of God

The Christian tradition has always acknowledged the mystery of God and the limits of human knowledge about God, but feminist theologians maintain that the persistent and exclusive use of male God language demonstrates an insufficient awareness of the mystery of God. No one name or set of names is adequate to understand God. A variety of names and images for God is not only acceptable, but necessary to reflect the fullness of God's character and activity. Scripture and tradition are much more varied in their language about God than is usually recognized.

The Bible reveals some truth about God, but it does not claim to have complete knowledge and, in fact, leaves many questions unanswered. The book of Exodus contains a fascinating story of an encounter between God and Moses. Moses was tending his sheep and minding his own business when God appeared in a burning bush and called Moses to liberate the Israelites from their slavery in Egypt. Moses replied that he would not be able to convince the Egyptian pharaoh to free his slaves. Moses could not simply arrive at the palace and announce that God wanted the people to be free. Pharaoh would want to know who this God was. Moses asked God for a definitive name to give to the skeptics and probably to himself.

God's answer did not provide the clarity Moses hoped for. It was vague, imprecise, indefinite. God said simply, "I am who I am." Another way to translate that is "I will be who I will be." God refused to be put in a box and precisely labeled with fancy terminology. "I am who I am" reminded Moses that God is mysterious, God cannot be fully known, God is always several steps ahead of human speculations. And yet this mysterious God chooses to help and be present with people. God cares for those God loves.

God is so mysterious and awesome that complete knowledge of God would overwhelm finite human beings. Late in his life Moses asked to see the glory of God. God replied that no one could see God's face and live; but after placing Moses in an opening in a rock wall, God covered Moses' face as God passed by, but permitted Moses a glimpse of God's back (Exod 33:18-23). Other biblical figures reported being overwhelmed or blinded when they encountered the presence of God (Isa 6:1-8). Such direct encounters seem relatively rare today. Human knowledge of God usually comes through Scripture, tradition, and experience, which means that knowledge is limited by human finitude and sin.

Theologians have tried to comprehend, speak, and write about this mystery, and at times their language multiplies words and concepts in dizzying ways. God is the "ground of all being," said Paul Tillich. Thomas Aquinas employed the term "unmoved mover." Hymn lyrics dating from the sixth century proclaim:

> High in the heavenly Zion Thou reignest God adored;
> And in the coming glory Thou shalt be Sovereign Lord.
> Beyond our ken Thou shinest, The everlasting Light;
> Ineffable in loving, Unthinkable in might.[9]

These words may offer a glimpse of God, but they too are incomplete because God is much more than words can express.

The theologians who speak and write at great length about God also recognize the limitations of their work. Augustine said, "If we have understood, then what we have understood is not God." And Thomas Aquinas wrote, "The supreme knowledge which we have of God is to know that we do not know God, insofar as we know that what God is surpasses all that we can understand of him."[10] A hymn writer addressed the mysterious God, "Immortal, invisible, God only wise, in light inaccessible hid from our eyes." Theological and devotional language may hint at the reality of God, but can never capture the essence or the fullness of God. Language is limited, as are the users of language. If we claim that God is limitless and transcendent, then we must also recognize that human language will not do justice to such a God.

The general caution of the Christian tradition regarding language for God does not extend to the use of male language. Most authors would admit that God is not really a male and God is not really a father; and yet they believe that God is more appropriately named in male terms. It seems natural and obvious since the Bible speaks of God as Father and he and because men have always possessed more power, respect, and authority than women. For many people in the tradition, Father has become God's name.

Feminist theologians argue that the exclusive use of any human term or characteristic for God can be a form of idolatry, which reduces the distance between the divine and the human by assuming that the divine can be adequately named in human terms. The frequent and casual use of the phrase "Father God" implies that God has been domesticated or tamed. Certainly God is like a father in some ways; but God is far more than that, and language for God ought to reflect a sense of mystery and awe as well as of relationship. Human beings ultimately cannot name the God who is always several steps ahead of them and who refuses to be confined to the names they choose.

Neither will God be confined by the trivial uses human beings often want to make of God's power and presence. Carter Heyward observed that we sometimes think of God as a big aspirin about whom it can be said, "Take a little God, you'll feel better." This God fixes all our problems for us, finds us parking spaces in crowded malls, and bails us out of tight situations. God gives clear guidance about every possible decision. Heyward suggests that it is far more biblical to think of God as enigmatic or incomprehensible. God is not in our control or at our beck and call. God does not exist to do our bidding or to make our lives more convenient. Often God does not make everything all better. Illness, pain, and death are not always fixable; but God is present in the midst of them.[11]

The assertion that language about God must be humble and cautious does not mean that knowledge of, or relationship with, God is impossible. Elizabeth Johnson concluded a discussion about the incomprehensibility of God by saying, "Ultimately, the highest human knowledge about God is to know that we do not know." Johanna Bos concluded a book about language for God with the statement that "The only 'wrong' naming of God is that which is sure of having it 'right.' " Elisabeth Schüssler Fiorenza wrote a prayer that included this paragraph:

> Our language is insufficient
> Our intellect does not grasp you
> Our imagination cannot get hold of you
> Although we do not know what to call you
> we are called by you.[12]

Recognizing human limits leads, not to despair, but to worship and awe.

Metaphor

If God is completely mysterious and incomprehensible, is it possible to say anything true about God? If human knowledge, comprehension, and language are limited, even damaged, how can we speak of God?

When Scripture speaks of God it rarely attempts to prove the existence of a divine being, but simply assumes that God is. The opening phrase of the Bible is "In the beginning when God created the heavens and the earth" (Gen 1:1). Scripture does not speak of God in abstract philosophical language, but describes God's actions in relationship to God's people. The authors use ordinary human language to make extraordinary claims about God. God is our rock, they proclaim. God is the light of the world. God gives birth to creation. God loves the people of Israel as a father loves his children. Scripture uses metaphors such as these to attempt to say something true about God. In the Gospel of Luke some religious people complained that Jesus spent too much time with tax collectors and sinners. In response, Jesus told three stories. God is like a shepherd searching for a lost sheep. God is like a woman searching for a lost coin. God is like a father welcoming home a lost son.

Metaphors are figures of speech that use something we know to explain something we do not know. We say clouds look like marshmallows, for example, because both are white and fluffy looking. Clouds are not exactly like marshmallows, however, because clouds are not small, edible, and made of corn syrup. Effective metaphors aid our understanding, but they are not literally true. When we use human experience to describe God as something like a mother, a father, or a rock, we qualify these comparisons because we recognize that God cannot be fully described by these images. The psalmist calls God a rock, which means that God is lasting and dependable; but God is not the small, rounded object I use to edge my garden. God is like a mother or a father in significant ways; but God is not harried, distracted, and short-tempered as human parents can be. Metaphors say something true about God, but they also remind us that divine reality far exceeds the metaphor.

Johanna Bos suggested the formula "yes, no, and more so" as a way to understand language for God. Many metaphors or names for God, such as Father, Mother, Rock, or Light, say something true about God—the "yes." Yet every metaphor falls short, and no title names God accurately or adequately—the "no." God always transcends human attempts to name and describe God—the "more so."[13] God is love, we often say, and it is true. But human understanding of love is limited, and God may be quite different from some of our notions of love. And yet God is more like love than we will ever know. God is love in a way that far exceeds our present knowledge of either God or love.

Language about God should help us to understand and encounter God, but we should not confuse the reality of God with the limits of our language. When my son was about nine months old, he enjoyed a book about bunnies. One day on a walk I said, "Look, Mark, there's a bunny," and I pointed at a rabbit. He looked quite intently at my finger, but had no idea that he was supposed to look beyond it to something else. Language should be like a finger pointing to the moon, Phyllis Trible wrote; but we often acknowledge the finger and not the moon, or we equate the two. We mistake our language about God for the reality of God, forgetting that language about God can never be more than an approximation.[14]

The most effective metaphors usually startle, shock, or surprise. When the Hebrew Scriptures occasionally referred to God as a father, or when Jesus prayed to God the Father, that was a fresh, surprising, even radical metaphor for God. Religious people usually thought of God as a distant being in the heavens. The biblical use of father imagery suggests a God who relates intimately with human beings, who is involved with them in a personal way, who is not isolated in heaven, but is connected with people as closely as a father to his children. Father language said something powerful and important about God, particularly where knowledge of biology was limited and people believed that the father was the primary source of life.

While it is completely understandable that a patriarchal society that did not value women very highly would think of God in male terms, it is not necessary for contemporary society to do so. Many feminist theologians argue that it is both unnecessary and idolatrous to use predominantly male language for God because it has lost much of its power to evoke meaning. Johanna Bos wrote, "If we conceive of the *father* metaphor as one which ascribes to God predominantly male attributes, we are in the realm of the dead metaphor. Worse than that, we are in the realm of idolatry." When metaphors become commonplace and obvious rather than surprising, they have lost the "and it is not" quality. When a human term ceases to be one way of understanding God and becomes God's real name, it has become an idol.[15]

Speaking of God so casually and frequently as he and Father, implies a belief that God is a male and that males more closely resemble God. When the man announced that if God the Father left the church, he was leaving also, he may have lost sight of the fact that Father is only a metaphor or symbol for God. The image of God the Father did not symbolize relationship and nurture for him, but was a weapon to be used in battle. When theologians insist that God is Father, not Mother, has Father become an idol?

Some Christians believe that Father is not simply a metaphor, but an actual name or title for God, revealed in Scripture as the appropriate way to address God. Many feminists would agree that father language can be an appropriate and meaningful way to speak of God, but insist that it cannot be the only way. The model of God as Father may be profound and true; but it is not the only model, and it does not render other models less true or profound.

The metaphorical language we use for God says something true about God, but not everything true. The Bible itself contains many metaphors for God; some are personal, some come from nature. Some of the most controversial have been those that are considered feminine.

Mother and Other Images for God

Consider some of the language the Bible uses for God's self-description. "For a long time I have held my peace,/ I have kept still and restrained myself;/ now I will cry out like a woman in labor,/ I will gasp and pant" (Isa 42:14). "Can a woman forget her nursing child,/ or show no compassion for the child of her womb?/ Even these may forget,/ yet I will not forget you" (Isa 49:15). "As a mother comforts her child,/ so I will comfort you;/ you shall be comforted in Jerusalem" (Isa 66:13).

In the second century Clement of Alexandria mixed his metaphors in his description of Christians nursing at the breast of God the Father. Medieval mystic Meister Eckhart described God's activity: "What does God do all day long? God gives birth. From all eternity God lies on a maternity bed giving birth."[16]

These excerpts from the Bible and from the history of Christianity suggest that imaging God as female is not a radical feminist innovation. People described God in feminine terms, not because God is actually a woman, but because feminine or maternal traits say something true about God and about their experience with God. Elizabeth Johnson wrote, "If women are created in the image of God, without qualification, then their human reality offers suitable, even excellent metaphor for speaking about divine mystery who remains always ever greater."[17]

Women's experience has provided several powerful biblical metaphors. Although these are admittedly not numerous, the fact that they appeared at all in a patriarchal culture is quite miraculous. Several biblical references speak of God giving birth to creation, laboring to create or bring the world into being. God is described as tenderly nurturing God's children, as in Hosea 11:1-9. Certainly a father could do this also, but the feeding and clothing of children would have been considered women's work in Israelite culture, as it usually is in ours. God is compared to a nursing mother. Just as she cannot forget her hungry child, so also God cannot forget or abandon the people of Israel.

God is compared to a mother hen in several psalms (57:1; 61:4; 91:4) where the author speaks of taking refuge under the shadow of God's wings. In his lament over Jerusalem in Matthew 23:37 and Luke 13:34, Jesus wishes to gather the city to himself as a hen gathers her chicks. The image suggests frightened chicks huddling within the warmth and safety of the mother bird's wings. It is interesting that when the image is used in a hymn, the pronoun is male: "Under his wings, I am safely abiding, there shall I hide till life's trials are o'er."

Christians cannot always hide under the wings of God because they are called to grow up, venture out, take risks. The image of God as mother eagle in Deuteronomy 32:11-12 and Exodus 19:4 offers a complement to the image of the hen. Virginia Mollenkott explained that when baby eagles are old enough to fly, the mother eagle begins nudging them out of the nest. She carries the baby eagles on her wings, then swoops out from under them to force them to fly on their own. But she is always present to catch them if they falter. This image of God encourages independence and action, rather than security and passivity. Both are important characteristics of God, who nurtures, enfolds, and comforts, but who also inspires bravery and self-confidence.[18]

Feminist theologians recognize that simply using feminine imagery for God does not resolve all the problems of God language. The Bible speaks of God as King, Judge, Creator, and many other traditionally male roles that are not linked to fathering. Much of the feminine imagery is maternal, which suggests that women are most like God when they are mothers, while men are like God in most of their activities. Maternal language about God can also become stereotypical. God the Mother is safe, warm, and gentle. God the Father is tough and demanding, but very strong and protective. God the Father is still clearly the boss. If the divine feminine is always linked with love and nurture, while the divine masculine is strong and rational, our stereotypes about male and female will be perpetuated rather than challenged.

The book of Hosea offers a useful antidote to stereotypical feminine imagery by portraying God as a female figure who is both maternal and furious. God faithfully fed and cared for the Israelites; but instead of being grateful, they forgot God. That made God say angrily, "I will fall upon them like a bear robbed of her cubs,/ and will tear open the covering of their heart" (Hos 13:8). This maternal image evokes no romanticized piety, softness, or sentimentality. Mothers, and the mother bear in Hosea, are fiercely protective. Elizabeth Johnson wrote of the paradox of angry love, "The wrath of God is a symbol of holy mystery that we can ill afford to lose. For the wrath of God in the sense of righteous anger against injustice is not an opposite of mercy but its correlative. It is a mode of caring response in the face of evil."[19]

Another nonmaternal feminine image is God as midwife, which occurs in Psalms 22 and 71. The psalmist described his feeling that God had abandoned him. His ancestors had trusted in God and were saved, but he felt God's scorn. In the midst of despair he said to God, "Yet it was you who took me from the womb;/ you kept me safe on my mother's breast./ On you I was cast from my birth,/ and since my mother bore me you have been my God" (Ps 22:9-10). He recognized that God had been present at the vulnerable time of birth, assuring his safety and comfort, and ever since. Comparing God to the one who helped deliver babies meant comparing God to a woman. It is an intriguing image, because midwives are active throughout a birth. They offer encouragement, they teach the mother how to work with the pains of labor; but they cannot do the laboring themselves, and they cannot take the pain away. The metaphor suggests that God encourages and supports human beings even when God cannot take their pain away.

These feminine images for God are meaningful, some feminists respond, but they are not sufficient to reverse the effects of several thousand years of male God language. The presence of a few Bible verses that compare God to a woman does not make Christianity or Judaism female friendly. Tinkering with the male symbols and images cannot change the fact that the word *God* evokes a male image in most people's minds because for years they have heard God named he and seen God portrayed in art and in other symbols as an old man with a beard and a long robe. Ascribing feminine traits to God may give the powerful, all-knowing deity the ability to be nurturing and compassionate, but a man with well-integrated feminine traits is still a man.

Some feminists believe that women can only be fully nurtured and affirmed by a female deity. Only then will women feel that they are fully in God's image. Several scholars have studied ancient cultures and found evidence of belief in and worship of female deities or goddesses. In her book *Rebirth of the Goddess,* Carol Christ included several pictures of goddess figures, some dating from 25,000 years ago. They have very large breasts, hips, and thighs, emphasizing procreation, but also strength and substance. These goddesses and others throughout history are valued as powerful, intelligent, independent women. They are thought to have creative powers. They assist in fertility and childbirth. They help the crops to grow and protect people from danger.

Christ recalled reading Christian theologians who believed that women were irrational and unable to control their passions. She could not reconcile this with her own experience.

> Gradually, it began to dawn on me that the image of God as Father, Son, and Spirit was at the root of the problem. No matter what I did, I would never be "in his image." While I had hoped to find in God a father who would love and accept my female self, it seemed that "he," like my father and most of my professors, liked boys better. I decided that unless we could call God Mother as well as Father, Daughter as well as Son, women and girls would never be valued.

Christ found herself increasingly alienated from God and from traditional religion. After one experience of pouring out her anger before God she heard a voice that said, " 'In God is a woman like yourself. She shares your suffering.' "[20] This experience marked the beginning of Christ's efforts to rediscover the role of goddess in ancient cultures and in contemporary women's lives. Worshiping a male God made some women distrust their own bodies and minds. Worshiping the goddess celebrated women's power, bodies, will, and connections with other women.

The rediscovery of the goddess has been a controversial element within feminism and religion. Christian critics charge that women want to discover the goddess in order to avoid dealing with a transcendent, powerful, demanding God who expects obedience. Worshiping a deity who is like women seems too easy. Goddess worship affirms and comforts women, but does not challenge them. Critics have also occasionally labeled all Christian feminists as goddess worshipers when that is clearly not the case. The use of feminine imagery to refer to the "I am who I am" of the Bible is not the same as worshiping the goddess. Similar benefits can result from both approaches, however, because many women feel far less alienated from a divine being who resembles them and in whose image they are created. Male critics who dismiss this need as irrelevant and irreverent often forget that there has never been any question that men are created in God's image.

Some Christian feminists are not convinced that a recovery of the goddess is the solution to the problem of God language. They point out that goddess religion tends to emphasize stereotypically feminine activities, such as giving birth and nurturing. The actual images of the goddess highlight, even exaggerate, women's distinctive sexual organs. Goddess religion may glorify women's bodily experience while neglecting other aspects of women's lives, such as the intellect and the vocation. Envisioning God as a woman or a goddess threatens to limit God to one image and exclude men just as women have been excluded for so long.

Many Names

When I teach about language for God in adult education programs or in college, I often ask my students to think of words that could be used to describe or image God. They generate an entire chalkboard full of thoughtful and creative names, masculine, feminine, natural, and biblical. Simply reading over the list evokes a sense of awe. Then I ask how many of those words are actually used in their worship experience, and we circle Father, King, Lord, and a few others. The words used regularly in worship are 10 to 15 percent of the words that might be used.

Brian Wren, a British hymn writer, regularly uses feminine imagery in his hymns, but he also introduces a variety of images for God that are not gender related.

> God of many Names
> gathered into One
> in your glory come and meet us,
> Moving, endlessly Becoming.
> God of Hovering Wings,
> Womb and Birth of time,
> joyfully we sing your praises,
> Breath of life in every people.
> God of Wounded Hands,
> Web and Loom of love,
> in your glory come and meet us,
> Carpenter of new creation.[21]

Using many names for God is valuable because each name, while saying something true about God, also has its limitations. The more names we use, the more likely we are to encounter the fullness and the mystery of God. Exclusively male or female language for God does not accurately represent God, since God is neither male nor female, but transcends gender. Exclusively transcendent language speaks truthfully about the distant elusiveness of God, but neglects the comforting, sometimes invasive presence of the immanent God. Exclusively immanent language speaks truthfully of God's participation in human life, but forgets that God is not a personal valet but participates in all human lives and in the world.

A similar problem exists with the use of parental language for God. The images of God as mother or father speak truthfully about relationship, care, and love. Used exclusively, they can foster an excessive sense of dependence and immaturity if the "children" of God are never encouraged to grow up. Sallie McFague, in her book *Models of God*, described the model of God as mother as a meaningful and valid way to speak of God, but she also encouraged the model of God as friend. This metaphor does not automatically evoke a gendered image, since people have friends of both sexes. Friendship is a mutual relationship, freely chosen. Friends support and encourage one another, recognizing that at times each friend will need to receive more or give more. Thinking of God as friend means that human beings are not always or only children in relationship to God, but are called to be responsible and to work along with God in the quest for justice and the reign of God.[22]

The model of God the Friend has its own limitations. It suggests a kind of equality between God and humanity that may not fully express God's distance and difference. It could limit God to a human level and fail to take seriously the mystery of God because human beings do not ordinarily worship their friends. McFague acknowledges the validity of these criticisms, but argues that God the Friend is still a truthful and meaningful image for God when considered alongside other images.

Another approach to the problem of God language emphasizes the activity of God. Mary Daly used the phrase "God the Verb," to point out that God should not be limited to static nouns when God is always acting and moving. More recently Gail Ramshaw spoke of God's power to act and to make a difference in the world. She suggested that one way to expand our language and illustrate God's involvement is to triple the verbs used for God. A reading of Exodus 3 suggests that God sees, hears, rescues, and cares about human suffering. The prophets suggest that God nurtures, guides, feeds, leads, and protects. Ramshaw noted that as science has found natural explanations for many events, there seems to be less of a need for God in the world. God does not cause the rain that makes the crops grow; a weather pattern does. Ramshaw maintained that worship and God talk that recognize the many ways God works in human life shows a lively faith.[23]

Conclusions

As I complete this chapter I am teaching a seminar on feminist theology. We are reading Elizabeth Johnson's book *She Who Is,* and my students are wrestling with the implications of feminine language for God. For twenty years they called God he and Father, and they picture God as an old white man with a beard and a long robe. Some of the women in the class never saw this as a problem. Now Johnson suggests that those images of God are insufficient, and Mary Daly argues that male God language is offensive and alienating. The question of God language challenges some of our deepest convictions and assumptions about who God is and how God relates to the world, but Johnson's and Daly's insights can be life-giving to contemporary Christianity.

Women are created in God's image, and women's experience can be used to speak of God. God is not offended or degraded by being described in feminine imagery. Feminist theologians are not creating God in their own image, but recovering feminine images of God from Scripture and tradition and developing new images. Discovering the feminine face of God has empowered women to discover their own value and strength and the worth of female experience.[24]

More broadly, the feminist discussion of God language reminds the Christian tradition of the vastness and mystery of this being we call God. Anne Carr described the feminist critique of male God language as "a powerful grace for theology and for the church in our time. It challenges a pervasive idolatry that has crept into Christian thought and practice and at the same time provides new awareness, for women and for the whole church, of God as the fully transcendent mystery who encompasses *all* of creation, *all* of our lives in universal presence."[25]

Recognizing the mystery of God requires a corresponding humility. Johanna Bos asked if contemporary Christians could admit that "no matter what our position—feminist, traditionalist, or in between—in speaking about God we are going to have it wrong?" Human words, no matter how eloquent or learned, are a "stammering approximation of the reality that is God. . . . What counts is not our proficiency in God-talk but our need, our thirst and hunger for the divine presence. For that need, God has abundant response."[26]

The last verse of Brian Wren's hymn entitled "Bring Many Names" expresses some of the paradox of the God who is both distant and near.

> Great, living God, never fully known,
> joyful darkness far beyond our seeing,
>   closer yet than breathing,
>   everlasting home:
> Hail and Hosanna,
> great, living God![27]

Or as Shug put it in *The Color Purple*, "People think pleasing God is all God care about. But any fool living in the world can see it always trying to please us back. . . . It always making little surprises and springing them on us when us least expect."[28] This is the amazing mystery. The immortal, invisible God is also the one in whom we live and move and have our being. The God who nurtures human beings under her wings is the God who encourages them to fly. She who is immutable and omniscient delights in the joy of her people. The almighty father tenderly caresses the cheeks of his children. The awesome, mysterious, transcendent God cares deeply about the world.

CHAPTER 4

Human Nature and Sin

Imagine yourself a wise, insightful person who has been asked to substitute for the vacationing Ann Landers and give advice on the following problems.

A college senior writes, "I've been accepted to a top-flight medical school in Pennsylvania, but I'm also very much in love with someone who has a job offer in Kansas City. I don't know whether to get married or go on to school."

A thirty-five-year-old executive says, "I'm really struggling. I love my work, but I don't get to spend enough time with my children. This job requires so much travel and quite a bit of overtime. I've been thinking about cutting back to part-time, but that doesn't seem like good stewardship of my education and experience."

A social worker writes, "I am so angry I don't know what to do. The governor has cut welfare benefits again, and my clients are really suffering. Those children and their moms don't have enough to eat, and they can't get decent housing. And yet the state is offering big tax cuts for the wealthy!"

What advice would you give? Did you notice that gender was never mentioned? Would it matter whether the pre-med student was Brian or Brianne; whether Chris, the executive, was Christopher or Christine? Would it seem odd for a male student to give up medical school for marriage? Would you advise an executive/mother to give up her job but not an executive/father? Would anger at injustice be more acceptable in a man than in a woman?

Or consider the following discussion about candidates for church leadership.

73

"Jack would be a fine elder. He is direct, straightforward, a real take-charge kind of guy. He always has something to say in Sunday school. He is a leader. He knows what the church needs, and he will make it happen."

"Barbara would be a fine elder. She is such a caring person. She would help the young mothers. And she is so easy to get along with. She never argues or refuses a task."

"Tim . . . I'm not so sure about him. He could not attend the men's retreat last month because his wife was on call that weekend. In worship committee meetings he always asks everyone for their opinion. He has done a great job teaching the first graders, but I'm not sure he has the leadership qualities to be an elder."

"Sarah . . . definitely not! She is so outspoken, aggressive, even angry sometimes. I've heard her confront the pastor more than once when she disagreed with him. And she always has something to say in the Bible study. She is much too bossy to be an elder."

This conversation suggests that there are different standards of behavior for men and women. Assertiveness is a virtue in a man and a vice in a woman. Assertive men are go-getters; assertive women are bossy. A direct and outspoken woman is criticized; a man is praised for the same behavior. A patient, generous, family man might be complimented at a Sunday school banquet, but criticized at work for inadequate commitment to his job. A church interviewing a female candidate wonders if the job is too much for the mother of three children, but does not ask the same question of a male candidate.

Gender roles are one of the most significant issues in contemporary culture and religion. How are men and women supposed to behave? The success of Promise Keepers shows that many Christian men are reconsidering their roles as husbands and fathers. During the last three decades the women's movement has challenged traditional notions of women's roles and attempted to expand the place of women. Conservative voices emphasize the importance of women remaining at home to care for young children.

The relationships between men and women are as complicated as their roles. If men are from Mars and women from Venus, how do they talk, work, and live together? How do they work together as equals when women have been the secretaries for so many years? How do women get beyond the glass ceiling without men feeling discriminated against? Can people who work together date? How does the military, with its hierarchical male culture, adapt to the presence of women?

Underlying these questions are deeper issues about what it means to be male and female and, more broadly, what it means to be human. This chapter will explore some biblical, historical, and psychological reflections about human nature and sin as well as Christian feminists' critiques of the traditional views and their efforts to rethink these concepts.

Women in the Bible and the Christian Tradition

The biblical stories about women, especially in Genesis 1–3, have profoundly affected the Christian understanding of male and female. There are two accounts of creation in the book of Genesis. The first, Genesis 1:1–2:4, records God's activity in each of the six days of creation, making light, sky, earth, plants, birds, fish, and animals. On the sixth day "God created humankind in his image,/in the image of God he created them;/male and female he created them" (Gen 1:27). And God pronounced it good.

The second account reports that before creating the plants and animals, God took the dust of the ground, formed a human being, and breathed life into it. The Hebrew word is *adham*, a generic term for a human being, rather than a proper name. God decided it was not good for this person to be alone, so God created all the animals; but none of them proved to be a suitable partner for the person. Then God put the human to sleep, took a rib, and made the rib into a woman.

Readers of these deceptively simple accounts of profound divine activity have produced many imaginative interpretations. In the fourth century Augustine argued that man was created directly in the image of God, but woman was only indirectly in God's image since she was created from the man's rib.

> The woman together with her own husband is the image of God, so that the whole substance may be one image; but when she is referred to separately in her quality of helpmate, which regards the woman herself alone, then she is not the image of God; but as regards the man alone, he is the image of God as fully and completely as when the woman too is joined with him.[1]

In the thirteenth century Thomas Aquinas conceded that the most important aspect of the image of God, the intellect, appeared in both men and women. But he also believed that men possessed the image of God in a way that women did not, "for man is the beginning and end of woman; as God is the beginning and end of every creature."[2]

A fifteenth-century book of instructions for hunting witches provides an amazing example of reading an agenda into the text. The authors wrote that women were "feebler both in mind and body," with a child-like intellect that could not understand philosophy. Women possessed character defects, such as weak faith, insatiable lust, and compulsive lying, because the first woman had been created from a bent rib. "And since through this defect she is an imperfect animal, she always deceives." These character traits did not arise out of sin, but out of female nature. The authors were so intent on rationalizing their persecution of women that they never asked why God created such defective creatures.[3]

Many men believed that women had only minimal intellectual capacity, but some men considered it dangerous for them to use what little ability they had. In thirteenth-century France, Philippe of Navarre wrote that "women should not learn to read or write unless they are going to be nuns, as much harm has come from such knowledge." He believed that men might write notes luring women into immoral liaisons, which they would not be able to resist.[4] In the nineteenth century some people believed that women who used their brains for education and scholarship drew energy from the uterus and made themselves sterile.

Women with such grave defects obviously needed someone to lead and guide them, and some readers found in the creation story clear evidence of what might be called a happy hierarchy. The man was created first to exercise headship over the woman, and woman was designed to be man's helpmate, to cook his food, wash his clothes, and bear his children. This is her purpose in life. She does not need an education because she will not have a public role, and she cannot exercise authority over men. As long as the woman accepted the man's headship, she was perfectly happy. When she did not, sin entered the world.

Genesis 2:16-17 records God's command that the human being could eat from any tree in the garden except the tree of the knowledge of good and evil. Genesis 3 reports that a crafty serpent entered the garden and told the woman that the tree would make her like God and give her the knowledge of good and evil. So she took some of the fruit and shared some with the man who was with her.

This story has also spawned numerous interpretations. One of the most common is that Eve was a stupid and gullible woman who was tricked by the serpent when she wandered away from her wise husband. When she realized what she had done, she used her feminine wiles to seduce her husband and trick him into eating the fruit. In the second century Tertullian charged all women with the responsibility for Eve's sin.

> Do you not know that you are Eve? God's sentence hangs still over all your sex and His punishment weighs down upon you. You are

the devil's gateway; you are she who first violated the forbidden tree and broke the law of God. It was you who coaxed your way around him whom the devil had not the force to attack. With what ease you shattered that image of God: man! Because of the death you merited, the Son of God had to die.[5]

Augustine was a bit kinder to women. He thought that women, like children or mentally ill people, could not be held responsible for the fall because their brains were insufficiently developed. John Chrysostom, on the other hand, wrote in the fourth century that women were not only responsible for the fall, but should be permanently punished for their actions.

The woman taught once, and ruined all. On this account...let her not teach. But what is it to other women that she suffered this? It certainly concerns them; for the sex is weak and fickle....The whole female race transgressed.[6]

These examples illustrate the dominant portrayal of women in the Christian tradition. In their created state women were defective, limited, and not quite in the image of God. In their sinful, fallen state women were seductive, manipulative, and disobedient temptresses. As an antidote to this grim diagnosis, the church fathers offered the positive role model of Mary, the innocent, virginal, obedient mother of Jesus. Unfortunately, the combination of virgin and mother was and is impossible for ordinary women to emulate.

During the Middle Ages most women had three vocational options: prostitute, wife, or virgin. The prostitute was openly sexual. Men might appreciate her services, but certainly didn't respect her, and the church considered her hopelessly sinful.[7] The wife was permitted to be sexual for the purpose of procreation, but her body was controlled by her husband. Virginity was the best choice, in the eyes of the church, because virgins devoted all their time and energy to God without the distractions of the body or children. Men could find an identity as a bricklayer, artist, scholar, or priest; but most women[8] were defined solely by their sexuality or lack of it. Their virtue and value consisted not in their contributions to the world's welfare or knowledge, but in the fact that their sexuality was under control.

What about women's intellect, soul, and emotions? Are women full persons and fully human in the same way as men? It did not seem so in much of the Christian tradition. Women have had to defend their humanity, prove their ability to reason and to manage their own lives, and answer charges that they caused sin in the world. Women could improve their status a bit via motherhood and even more via the convent and virginity, but they were rarely recognized as simply and fully human.

Our culture has often claimed that women can be either innocent or evil, but not fully human. In the movie *Snow White and the Seven Dwarfs*, the two female roles illustrate the characterization of women as Eve or as Mary. Snow White is beautiful, kind, loving, and a hardworking cook and housekeeper. The forest animals adore her, and upon seeing her for the first time, the prince falls instantly in love. She is both a maternal presence and a chaste romantic figure to the dwarfs, who are so enamored with her that they even wash! Her high-pitched voice makes her sound about six years old and not exceptionally bright. She is far too nice and trusting for her own good. In contrast, the queen, her stepmother, is beautiful in a hard and frightening way. She is cruel, jealous, vindictive, and definitely not a maternal presence for Snow White. The queen uses magical powers to transform herself into an ugly beggar woman and make a poison apple for Snow White to eat.

This movie is sixty years old and reflects a very different cultural context, but its long-term popularity suggests that its underlying themes continue to entrance. Snow White is the ideal woman: maternal, chaste, domestic, and beautiful. The stepmother embodies common fears about women because she is full of "womanly wiles" that are out of control. Several Disney movies present the same two opposite views of women: Anita and Cruella de Vil in *101 Dalmatians*, Cinderella and her stepmother and stepsisters, and Ariel and Ursula in *The Little Mermaid* all come to mind as examples. In these fairy tales the Disney animators and storytellers vividly illustrated the forces we fear and the traits we admire. They did not create these archetypes; they have existed for centuries.[9]

A modern version of the Eve and Mary characterizations appeared in the movie *Fatal Attraction*. The evil single woman tempted the weak husband to sin, then tormented him and his faithful wife. Similarly, in soap operas women characters are often categorized either as nice women who are a little boring or as evil women who make things happen. Hillary Rodham Clinton was frequently characterized as bossy, demanding, and a bad presidential wife when she worked on health care reform. Many people seem to like her much better in her role as mother, author, and goodwill ambassador.

Whether in the media, in music videos, or in politics, the image of women as either good or evil presents a very simplistic and flat portrait. Women are not angels or demons, wives or witches, saints or sinners, but complex mixtures of the various vices and virtues common to all human beings.

Feminist Critique and Re-visioning: What Does It Mean to Be Human?

Old Testament scholar Phyllis Trible wrote a groundbreaking essay in 1973 that reviewed many of the common interpretations of Genesis 2–3 and noted how few of them were supported by the text.[10] For example, many interpreters have explained that woman is a helpmate to the man, which means she has a secondary role of assisting him in his vocation by cooking, cleaning, and caring for his children. Trible argued that this is a distortion of the text. The word help or *ezer*, is most often used for God, as in "My help comes from the Lord, who made heaven and earth" (Ps 121:2). An *ezer* is a strong and powerful help. Instead of helpmate, the Hebrew should be translated as a "help appropriate for him." The phrase certainly does not describe a submissive wallflower.

A second misinterpretation is that God created man first, which made him more important or at least more nearly in God's image. Trible responded that the order of creation implied absolutely no hierarchy. If it did, then according to Genesis 1, humanity should be subordinate to the animals, fish, and birds, which were created before them. Trible described the literary format of Genesis 2–3 as ring structure in which the most important points, the creation of the two human beings, were located in the most literary positions at the beginning and the end. Woman was not an afterthought to keep the man happy, but the culmination of God's creative efforts.

Trible and other feminist theologians have also pointed out that the Genesis 1 account clearly states that both male and female were created in God's image. There is no evidence in the biblical texts that women possessed fewer intellectual, physical, or moral abilities. There is no hierarchy, happy or otherwise, and there is no division of labor by gender. God told both to be fruitful and multipy and gave to both dominion over the animals (Gen 1:28-30). The conclusions drawn by church fathers that women were made from a bent rib or are otherwise inferior are not grounded in the biblical text.

Feminist theologians also point out that both the Bible and the Christian tradition contain positive and wholistic examples of women's lives. Women were occasionally portrayed as faithful, intelligent, and spiritually mature. Deborah was a prophet and a judge in Israel, respected for her wise counsel. When Barak was told to go into battle, he refused to go unless Deborah went with him. After they won, an Israelite victory song praised Deborah as a mother in Israel (Judg 4–5).

The Gospel of Matthew tells the story of a foreign women who asked Jesus to heal her daughter. He responded rather coldly to her, "I was sent only to the lost sheep of the house of Israel." When she again begged for help he said, "It is not fair to take the children's food and throw it to the dogs." Rather than simply accept his refusal, she replied, "Yes, Lord, yet even the dogs under the table eat the crumbs that fall from their masters' table." Jesus was deeply affected by her faith and promised that her daughter would be healed. This woman encouraged Jesus to broaden his ministry beyond Jews to include Gentiles as well, in part because she demonstrated the depth of her own faith (Matt 15:21-28).

Lioba was an abbess in the eighth century who assisted in the evangelization of Germany and was respected for her virtue and her teaching. In the fourteenth century Catherine of Siena gave advice to popes, and they listened. In the sixteenth century Katherine Zell, a minister's wife, was known for her theological insight, hospitality, and care for the poor. In spite of the opinions of the church fathers that women were intellectually and spiritually deficient, some women effectively exercised authority in church and society, used their considerable intellects, and fought social expectations in order to live out the vocation to which God had called them.[11]

Given this ambiguous legacy from the Bible and the Christian tradition, feminist theologians have asked what it means to be a woman when for so long women have been considered secondary, deficient, and less than fully human. They also ask broader questions about what it means to be human and how men and women are alike and different.

Essentially the Same or Different?

One of the most obvious forms of human diversity is that of *sex*. To be one sex or the other means to have certain physical characteristics. To be a man or a woman involves more than the body, so we speak of *gender* as those characteristics or behaviors that cultures have labeled masculine or feminine. Masculine, for example, is often equated with being tough, macho, athletic, and independent; and feminine, with being sweet, nurturing, passive, and dependent, although different cultures define masculine and feminine in different ways. The meanings of masculine and feminine gender are not as obvious as the physical differences of sex, and they must be learned. Some people believe that gender roles are deeply rooted in human nature, so that women have an instinct for nurturing and men have an instinct for aggression just as some animals have an instinct for hibernating in the winter. Some people believe that the Bible teaches the proper roles. Others argue that human beings are socialized by their parents, schools, and culture to behave in certain ways. In all of these debates over how people learn to be men and women, there is a more basic question: How different are men and women?

Two explanations for the similarities and differences of men and women have emerged in psychological and religious literature. The first emphasizes the differences and claims that men and women actually have two different natures. The second emphasizes the similarities, arguing that men and women share the same nature and differ only in the biological structure and capacity of their bodies.

Drawing from the account of creation in Genesis 2, the two-nature theory emphasizes the fact that men and women have very different bodies and reproductive tasks, but also more subtle differences. Men have more testosterone, women have more estrogen. Men are often physically stronger and more aggressive than women. Women tend to be physically weaker and less aggressive. From these biological tendencies many people have concluded that "anatomy is destiny" and that male or female sex determines what kind of person we will be, what we will be good at, even our vocation in life.

The two-nature theory seems to explain some persistent patterns in human nature. Despite our best efforts to raise our son without gender stereotypes, at three he announced that dolls were for girls and basketball was for boys. Our five-year-old daughter delights in nurturing younger children. The two-nature theory suggests that they are living out the biological destiny that is established for them before birth. Women are programmed to be nurturers, men to compete in sports and business.

The two-nature theory also takes account of the ways biological differences shape human lives. The presence of a uterus gives women the potential for childbearing that men can never experience, but women can also be raped or become pregnant when they do not want to be. Women's biology makes them more vulnerable to violence and pain. Two-nature theorists argue that this vulnerability makes women yearn for the protection of a stronger man.

Although the two-nature theory appears to explain some of human experience, it is also deficient in several ways. There are many exceptions to the claim that anatomy is destiny. The fact that some mothers neglect, abuse, and even murder their children shows that the presence of a uterus does not make women naturally nurturing. The large number of kind, caring men in the world shows that the presence of testosterone does not make all men naturally aggressive. Despite the stereotype that men think and women feel, there is no clear connection between male sex and rationality or between female sex and intuition.

Gender roles vary across cultures, which suggests that neither God

81

nor biology has determined what is "natural" for all men and women. The most universal pattern is that men perform the tasks deemed interesting or powerful in the community and delegate to women the dull and repetitive work. The feeding and diapering of children has rarely been granted much status in any culture and thus is regularly given to women as their particular vocation.[12] Similarly, the Bible does not specify that men should be rational and aggressive and women emotional and nurturing. Biblical writers made no sweeping pronouncements about the way all men or all women should act.

Another weakness of the two-nature theory is that even some of the most persistent myths about men and women have begun to change. This suggests that most gender roles are not natural, but socially constructed. Gender roles may have a connection with the body, but the roles have often been developed far beyond the obvious physical rationale. For example, since women give birth and breast feed they may be more closely connected with infants in the first year of life; but once a child is weaned, that connection is no longer required. A father has equal capacity to care for children. The assumption that women are primarily responsible for all child care is a decision that societies make, not a rule of nature.

The single-nature theory draws on the creation account in Genesis 1, asserting that human nature takes one basic form rather than two. Men and women are far more alike than different and share the human characteristics of reason, emotion, body, and spirit. Both need meaningful work and relationships. Human beings are very diverse, but the differences are not divided neatly along gender lines. Sometimes two people of opposite sex are similar in temperament and ability, while two people of the same sex are completely different in personality and interests.

Single-nature theorists recognize the existence of gender differences, but attribute them to socialization rather than to biology. At birth infants are placed in hospital bassinets labeled with a pink or a blue name card. Baby girls receive dozens of pink outfits and ruffled dresses. Baby boys receive blue outfits and footballs. Adults play more roughly with boys and talk more to infant girls about their appearance. Little girls are not born caretakers, but learn to be by watching their mothers, observing cultural cues, and being affirmed for nurturing. Little boys are not naturally aggressive, but learn to be by playing war games, being told that big boys don't cry, and hearing an amused adult say, "Isn't he all boy?" Television is a powerful force of socialization. Did my son know that dolls are for girls because it was an innate biological rule or because television ads always show girls playing with them? The encouragement of parents and other adults also shapes a child's sense of gender roles.

Does my daughter like to put her dolls to bed because it is her nature or because her grandmother brought out the old doll beds from my childhood, which she had not done for our son?

One of the most important socialization experiences occurs in early childhood. For the last two centuries small children have spent most of their time with their mothers, while many fathers worked away from the home and had only a minimal presence in their children's lives. Little boys may not be entirely sure what it means to be a man, but they learn that becoming a man means differentiating themselves from the mother. To be a man is to be not like a woman and to have a different role than the strong maternal presence. Little girls, on the other hand, grow up without needing to separate completely. They can continue to relate to and imitate their mothers. This psychological theory may help to explain some of the persistent patterns of greater autonomy in men and relationality in women.[13] It will be interesting to see whether changes occur now that some fathers are more involved in the lives of infants and small children.

Some two-nature theorists suggest that the large number of male engineers, scientists, and presidents proves that men have greater scientific, mathematic, and leadership abilities. The number of female nurses, elementary school teachers, and secretaries shows that women possess helping skills that men do not. They point to standardized test scores that seem to indicate that girls excel at language; and boys, at mathematical and spatial skills. Single-nature theorists argue that there is little evidence that proves that these patterns are linked to male and female sex. Testosterone does not guarantee mathematical ability. It is far more likely that educational expectations have directed boys toward science and math and girls toward the humanities and the helping professions. Male or female sex does not determine ability as much as do the children's books that portray Johnny as a doctor and Sally as a nurse, the preponderance of women elementary school teachers, and the guidance counselors who steer girls into English and boys into physics.[14]

The single-nature theory emphasizes human freedom and responsibility rather than biological determinism. Men and women are not assigned to one role, but are equally able to care for children, think, lead, make decisions, and contribute to the welfare of society. Both women and men are equally responsible to use the abilities God has given them. Some proponents of the two-nature theory argue that women who work outside the home and use day care are selfish, greedy, and uncaring. Working fathers, on the other hand, are never blamed for the moral decline of society. The underlying assumption is that men are "supposed" to work and women are "supposed" to care for children; but it is society that determines this, not biology or nature.

The single-nature theory also has its limitations. Its emphasis on sameness and equality tends to downplay the role of the body, making it little more than a vehicle for procreation. The body and sexuality affect all of human life, not just the procreation event; thus the single-nature theory may not pay enough attention to the differences men and women experience regarding their bodies.

The single-nature theory fails to adequately account for diversity, if it assumes that all human beings are the same, or should be, because of their common nature. Variations in race, class, gender, social location, and sexual orientation combine to yield abundant diversity. If historians assume that they need to tell only the story of white American men because all people are the same anyway, they falsely reduce human experience to the experience of a few. If people argue that affirmative action is no longer necessary because everyone is equal and we are all human beings, they disregard centuries of inequity. The single-nature theory cannot be used as a rationale for the argument that everyone is the same.

There is no single feminist opinion about human nature. Some feminists emphasize the role of the body; others, the role of socialization. Some feminists argue for a single human nature; others, that there are two natures and that female nature is more peaceable, caring, and connected than is male nature. All feminists believe that female nature is good, rational, and fully human. Women are not merely bodies, baby machines, or household servants, but complete persons with minds and souls and the capacity for leadership and authority as well as for nurturing. The full humanity of women should not require debate or defense because, as Daphne Hampson noted about the struggle for women's ordination, "To be forced to argue that one is a full human being of equal dignity (for that is what it felt like) is quite extraordinarily undermining."[15] The teachings of the Christian tradition have been ambiguous and even undermining at times, but Christian feminists believe that at heart the Bible affirms women as created in God's image and therefore as fully human. They also experience the limits and brokenness that the Christian tradition calls sin.

Sin

Despite the fact that human beings do many good things and reflect the image of God in remarkable ways, it is equally clear that people are not always good. Human beings do unspeakable things to each other, sometimes in the name of the God who created them. How did people created in God's image become so broken? How did the image of God become so distorted?

The worst examples of evil—the Holocaust, the Oklahoma City bomb-ing, the senseless murder of a friend—demand our attention and beg for answers; but brokenness and distortion occur in all parts of human lives. It is all too easy to be cranky with family members, to be selfish or lust-ful or arrogant. We convince ourselves that the wrong thing is really the right thing. Why is sin so persistent and prevalent?

Traditional Christian theology asserts that sin arises out of human pride, egoism, disobedience, and desire. Adam and Eve disobeyed God by breaking the rules, much as a toddler deliberately tests and defies limits. Adam and Eve illustrate how pride and arrogance arise out of an inflated self that has enormous confidence in its own abilities and fails to acknowledge God. They wanted to gain the knowledge the fruit repre-sented, and they disregarded the limits God had set. Sin in these terms is primarily against God, although human relationships are also affected. Sin damages the relationship between God and the individual and mars the soul.

The sin of Adam and Eve affected all of humanity. It is as if they trans-mitted an ineradicable genetic disease to their descendants, who will inevitably sin. Theologians call this original sin. Even the best people have their broken places, and even those who put forth great effort find it difficult not to sin. Brokenness was not part of God's plan for creation, but is now an inescapable part of the human condition.

Feminist Critique and Revisioning: The Problem of Sin

Feminist theologians have challenged the traditional Christian under-standing of sin on a number of points. They do not deny the reality of sin, but they question the way sin has been defined and particularly the way it has been linked to women.

Blaming Eve

For centuries women have been seen as the cause of the world's trou-bles. Evil is often personified as female. Greek mythology tells of the beautiful Pandora who had a box of troubles that she released into the world. In the movie *Snow White and the Seven Dwarfs*, Grumpy, the skep-tical dwarf, said of Snow White: "She's a female, and females are poison. They're full of womanly wiles." "What are they?" another dwarf asked. "I don't know," Grumpy replied. "But whatever they are, I'm agin' 'em." C. S. Lewis sent a powerful, if unintended, message in *The Lion, The Witch, and the Wardrobe* when he portrayed the Christ figure Aslan as a powerful, loving, and male lion and the evil witch as a manipulative female. More recently, an advertisement for whiskey showed a happy bride and a miserable groom with the outline of a noose around his neck. The ad copy read, "Life as you know it may change. Your drink doesn't have to. Hang on to your spirit."

The quotations from the church fathers that appeared earlier in the chapter illustrate some of the ways that Eve has been disproportionately blamed for the fall of humanity. Both sinned, but Eve's sin has been considered worse than Adam's. The author of 1 Timothy did not permit women to teach or to have authority because Eve was deceived, but not Adam. In a commentary on Genesis Martin Luther wrote that the man rules the home and state. "The woman, on the other hand, is like a nail driven into the wall . . . the wife should stay at home and look after the affairs of the household, as one who has been deprived of the ability of administering those affairs that are outside and that concern the state."[16] Because of Eve's weakness, women must be controlled by and subordinate to their husbands. The Southern Baptist Convention stated this explicitly in 1984 when it pronounced that women could not be ordained and were cursed by God with permanent subordination because of their primary responsibility for sin.

Many feminist biblical scholars believe that these are inaccurate readings of the text. Phyllis Trible rehabilitated Eve, in a way, by suggesting that she was the more intelligent theologian. The tree offered good food and a source of wisdom, so she chose to eat it. "By contrast, the man is a silent, passive, and bland recipient. . . . The man does not theologize; he does not contemplate; he does not envision the full possibilities of the occasion." Trible also dismissed claims that the woman seduced the man into eating the fruit. There is no such language in the text, which simply reports that after a theological discussion with the serpent, the woman ate the fruit and gave some to her husband, who was with her. She did not seek him out and disguise the fruit by baking it into a pie, for example, thus giving it to him surreptitiously. They both knew what they were doing. They both made a choice that had profound consequences.[17]

Trible also reinterpreted the consequences of their action. The text says that the serpent is cursed, but the man and the woman are judged for their sin. Their actions had consequences. Painful childbirth, hard work, and a hierarchical relationship were not God's choice for humanity, but were the inevitable result of distorted relationships with God and with each other. The woman became a slave and the man became a master. They no longer lived in the equality and mutuality God intended.[18]

Feminist theologians and other scholars have argued that the story of the Fall should not be interpreted literally, but read as a story or a myth that explains the origins of human sinfulness. The purpose of the text was not necessarily to blame women for sin, but to interpret the brokenness that persisted between men and women, and humans and God. After Genesis 3 the Bible rarely refers to the Fall and instead describes the fundamental human sin in terms of the Israelites's disobedience to God and injustice to their neighbors. When Paul talks about the origins of sin, he refers to Adam rather than to Eve.

The story does offer a perceptive insight about the relationships between men and women: "Your desire shall be for your husband, and he shall rule over you" (Gen 3:16). Or, as a contemporary author phrased it, women tend to longing and men tend to lording.[19] Sexual desire can lead to painful childbirth; but, more broadly, women's deep care has sometimes led them to do or care too much for a man who does not reciprocate or to stay in a destructive or abusive relationship. He can be domineering, distant, and unresponsive; and he may find power in the fact that he does not need her as much as she needs him. Certainly not all, perhaps even most, relationships are like this; but the pattern exists often enough. Distorted, uneven relationships are not the result of God's will, but of human sinfulness.

Despite its realism about the brokenness caused by sin, Scripture does not blame Eve for all the sins of the world, although some of the church fathers did. After the Southern Baptist Convention denied women ordination because of the sin of Eve, Bill Leonard reflected that the action suggested an image of God who was forever getting even and whose grace was limited. "If the curse of Eve remains, then there are no really new creations. Old things will never pass away. If some people are too cursed to be called, they may be too cursed to be saved. If there is not enough grace for Eve, there may not be enough for the rest of us."[20] In the nineteenth century Sojourner Truth offered another way to respond to the charge that Eve was at fault for sin. She said, "If the first woman God ever made was strong enough to turn the world upside down all alone, these women together ought to be able to turn it back, and get it right side up again! And now they is asking to do it, the men better let them."[21]

Sin defined in terms of male experience

The second area in which the traditional view of sin has not been helpful to women is its definition in terms of male experience. In an essay published in 1960 Valerie Saiving reviewed the work of two contemporary theologians, Reinhold Niebuhr and Anders Nygren. They defined sin as pride, egoism, and self-love. Most of their predecessors in the Christian tradition agreed that sin consists of too much concern for self, or placing the self at the center of the universe. To remedy this sin they advocated self-giving love, which takes no thought for one's own needs.

Several years before anyone else asked such questions, Saiving wondered whether this understanding of sin is true to the experience of women, which is quite different from that of men. Girls are socialized to care for others, as their mothers did. Boys are socialized toward autonomy and independence, like their fathers. The nature of motherhood is to provide nurture and care without expecting much in return and without concern for one's own needs. Saiving suggested that the temptation for women is to think too much of others and to ignore themselves. She observed that women's sin is not so much pride and egoism as "triviality, distractibility, and diffuseness; lack of an organizing center or focus; dependence on others for one's own self-definition; tolerance at the expense of standards of excellence; inability to respect the boundaries of privacy; sentimentality, gossipy sociability, and mistrust of reason—in short, underdevelopment or negation of the self."[22] Forty years later, this list of sins seems a bit narrow, since clearly women can also be proud and self-serving; but Saiving's insight has been extremely influential. If many women lack a strong sense of self and care too much for others, it will not be helpful for them to hear that self-differentiation and self-confidence, the very characteristics they need to develop, are sinful.

Judith Plaskow wrote that sin for women could be the failure to center the self and take responsibility for one's life. "It can be said that women's sin, so far from being the sin of pride, lies in leaving the sin of pride to man." Jacquelyn Grant also protested the traditional Christian assumption that sin means pride and selfishness. "For women of color, the sin is not the lack of humility, but the sin is too much humility. Further, for women of color, the sin is not the lack of service, but too much service."[23] Certainly women can be proud and selfish, but many women find that the sins that haunt them are a lack of self-confidence and too much willingness to care for others. Women's experience and socialization may make them more vulnerable to sins of passivity, fear, and the reluctance to take a risk.

Some feminists have concluded that women sin, not only differently, but also less often, or in other words, that women are more virtuous and peaceable. Therese Souga wrote, "While under the domination of the male side of humankind, the universe tends to be harsh, closed, aggressive, and even unjust. The Christian woman, following Christ, is the bearer of harmony, sweetness, justice, and understanding. . . . she is responsible for inviting the man to have a different vision of reality."[24] Rosemary Radford Ruether disagreed:

The systems of domination, then, are "male" only in the historical and sociological sense that males have shaped and benefited from them, not in the sense that they correspond to unique, evil capacities of males that women do not share. Women have no guarantees, because of a different "nature," that they will act differently. They do have some different experiences that may help them avoid acting in the same way, but only if they can develop the grounded self that avoids both timidity and reversed egoism.[25]

Most Christian feminists believe that women sin differently than men do, but few are willing to say that women do not sin at all.

Sin has corporate, as well as individual, dimensions

Feminist theologians critique the individualistic definitions of sin that are so common in the Christian tradition. They agree that sin can be partially explained as a broken relationship with God or as wrong attitudes, such as lust, pride, and unbelief, but insist that sin affects all human relationships. Aruna Gnanadason described sin as the distortion of what should be a mutual relationship into one characterized by domination and control. "It can also be seen in women's passive acquiescence before such distortions. Therefore sin must be seen not merely as one individual personal straying away from the values of justice and peace but as a collective, systematic destruction of the community that is at the foundation of God's good creation."[26] Feminist theologians particularly name as sinful those actions against other human beings that the church has often ignored or downplayed, such as abuse, incest, and domestic violence. They have pointed out that not only the perpetrators are sinful, but also the individuals and institutions who enable such behavior, protect it with silence, or offer easy forgiveness without real repentance. Community is destroyed when people treat each other unfairly or fail to recognize the humanity of another person or group.

Feminist theologians acknowledge the persistent presence of structural and systemic sin, such as racism, sexism, and classism. Regina Coll explained, "Systemic sin is that sin which exists in the structures, institutions, customs, and laws of society. It is the sin for which no individual tends to feel responsible because it is the result of decisions, judgments, and actions of so many. It is the sin that results when reverence and respect for the human beings involved is missing."[27] Systemic sin or oppression occurs when one group of people has their feet on the necks of others, to use Sarah Grimke's image. Or as Letty Russell put it, sin is not giving others room to breathe.[28] Oppression occurs when "human beings attempt to play God over other human beings"[29] by refusing to allow them the right to determine the course of their own lives.

In the American South during the eighteenth and nineteenth centuries, preachers often chastised slaves for disobedience to their masters. Was that the real sin? Abolitionists in the North condemned the sin of slave-holding, but many of them were racist themselves and did not think that freed slaves deserved equal treatment in society or a seat next to them in church or school. Some Southern white women during this time protested the unequal treatment of women, but still owned and mistreated slaves. Enslaved black men fought against racism, but expected their wives to serve them. Sin has many layers and no one is exempt. Even those who are oppressed may deny others the room to breathe.

A Critique of Feminism: An Adequate Sense of Sin?

Critics have suggested that feminist theologians identify sin as sexism and men as sexists and thus blame sin on others without recognizing the sinfulness of women. They find sin in patriarchal structures but never in themselves. Critics have also argued that feminists overemphasize social sin and oppression and fail to see that individual sin is an offense against God that requires personal repentance. Feminist theologians have a superficial sense of sin, the critics claim, and do not understand that transforming social structures and eliminating patriarchy will never cure the deep sin rooted in individual hearts.

It is true that many feminist theologians are relatively optimistic about human nature. They emphasize the goodness present in God's creation and the many abilities human beings possess. They see the great potential in human beings, who are created in God's image. They believe that God cares deeply about people; wants them to find wholeness; and gives them the power to heal, survive, and change.

Feminist theologians emphasize social transformation more than individual repentance; but most of them recognize that sin is present in all people, including women. Chung Hyun Kyung described the difficult lives of Asian women who are oppressed in many ways by a sinful patriarchal system. She insisted, though, that these women do not consider themselves free of sin. They recognize their own passive obedience and failure to trust themselves and other women.[30] In recent years white feminists have been increasingly perceptive about their own racism and classism and the ways white middle-class women have sinned by perpetuating injustice among women of other races and classes.

Some feminists are more likely to describe sin as Rita Nakashima Brock does, as damage that needs healing. In contrast to the traditional doctrine of original sin, Brock wrote that

90

sinfulness is neither a state that comes inevitably with birth nor something that permeates all human existence, but a symptom of the unavoidably relational nature of human existence through which we come to be damaged and damage others. . . . Sin emerges because our relationships have the capacity to destroy us, and we participate in destruction when we seek to destroy ourselves or others. Hence sin is a sign of our brokenheartedness, of how damaged we are, not of how evil, willfully disobedient, and culpable we are. Sin is not something to be punished, but something to be healed.[31]

For Brock, sin is most accurately imaged, not as a stubborn child yelling no, but as a wounded child shrinking from harsh words or punishment. Sin is more like a terminal illness than a destructive self-chosen behavior.

Sally Purvis offered a useful definition of sin when she wrote,

Sin is to be understood as the incapacity to trust the power of love and thus the necessity to try to control relationships with and the behavior of others. . . . Sin, in this view, is not a set of inappropriate or illegal or immoral behaviors but the odd incapacity to love, to choose love, to trust love. . . . Sin is the painful, frustrating, damaging process of wanting to heal—oneself or another or a relationship—and of continuing to wound and to be wounded.[32]

The Bible often describes sin in terms of willfulness, as when the Israelites chose to follow other gods, or when the Corinthian Christians thumbed their noses at the weaker members of their community, or when religious legalists preferred rules over relationships. It is equally clear from Scripture that these behaviors arose from a deeply distorted understanding of life and relationships. The Israelites found it very difficult to trust God. The Corinthians needed to prove their superior Christian faith. The legalists found it safer to deal with a God of rules and regulations than with a God of surprising grace and mercy. Arrogant and willful behavior sometimes arises out of inadequacy, fear, and anxiety rather than out of pride. Even people who want to do good often do not, as expressed poignantly in Paul's awareness that despite his best intentions he chose to do evil rather than good (Rom 7:15).

Feminist theologians believe that sin pervades all human relationships and abilities. It damages self-confidence, it fosters pride and arrogance, it distorts what should be mutuality and trust into domination and subjection. God grieves for the ways that human beings distance themselves by rejecting or ignoring the divine presence, but God also grieves for the damage that human beings do to themselves and others. The failure to

91

regard one's self as a person created in God's image is a sin against God. The failure to regard another human being as a person created in God's image is a sin against God. The failure to fight against oppression and injustice is a sin against God. Sin exists in structures and individuals, in women and men, in good people and bad. Sin affects thought, actions, attitudes, and relationships. It is everywhere, but it does not have the last word.

CHAPTER 5

Christology

A cartoon drawing of a traditional manger scene showed the stable, the wise men, the star, and a few sheep. A voice from the stable announced, "It's a girl!"

Artist Edwina Sandys created a sculpture of a female form, arms outstretched as if hanging from a cross. The sculpture, entitled *Christa*, has created controversy wherever she is displayed. Critics say the statue defies the historical fact that Jesus was a man. Some viewers feel that the symbol of the cross is degraded or even blasphemed by a Christ in female form. Others are disturbed by the sexual overtones of the naked woman. Some people are troubled by yet another violent image of female suffering. A few people see in the sculpture the message that the death of Jesus symbolizes the pain of all human suffering.

The response to these visual images reveals various theological assumptions. Some people dismiss the cartoon and the sculpture because they are literally false. Jesus was a man. End of discussion. Other people consider these images offensive and uncomfortable. It insults Jesus, and them as well, to think of him as a woman. These imaginative reconstructions of important events in the life of Jesus pose an important theological question: What difference does it make that Jesus was male?

Some feminists conclude that if the central truth of Christianity is that God became a man, then men are to be considered superior to women. If the central figure of Christianity is a heroic male figure human beings must obey, worship, and adore in order to receive salvation, then this religious tradition is simply another example of a man telling women what to do, which cannot be good news for women. If a man is the most important figure in Christianity, then women can never be equal to men,

93

because if the starring role must be played by a man, women will always be limited to supporting roles.

The maleness of Jesus may seem so obvious that further discussion is irrelevant. Some of my students have asked, with more than a trace of irritation, "Jesus was a man. Why are we talking about this?" The historical reality of the maleness of Jesus cannot be questioned or even discussed without challenging the wisdom of God's plan. Christians must simply acknowledge that God had good reasons for taking on male flesh.

One such reason is that in a patriarchal culture a man was far more suited to be a leader, a prophet, and a teacher. A woman may not have had the freedom or the resources to travel. Her words and actions would not have been respected or even accepted. The cultural situation of the time permitted only a male Messiah.

Another explanation for the maleness of Jesus is that God the Father naturally and necessarily chose to reveal "himself" in male form, because God is a male and because maleness more adequately represented God. If women were biologically and intellectually defective and naturally in a state of subjection, as many theologians argued, then of course Christ had to take on male nature because female nature was not only inadequate, but unreasonable and even somewhat revolting.

Christian feminists have been unwilling to dismiss Christianity as completely without value, but neither can they accept without further discussion the claim that the maleness of Jesus was theologically necessary. This chapter will explore some of the ways in which feminist theologians have understood the life and work of Jesus in his own time and his continuing significance in the present.

Who Was Jesus?

There has never been a single understanding of or perspective on Jesus. Seventy years after his death and resurrection, four different Gospels or accounts of his life existed, each written for a specific audience and highlighting certain aspects of his life and ministry. Matthew wrote for Jewish readers and emphasized the way Jesus fulfilled prophecies from the Jewish Scriptures. Mark wrote for Christians who experienced persecution and emphasized the suffering of Jesus. Luke wrote for a gentile or non-Jewish audience and stressed that the message of Jesus was for the whole world. John was written somewhat later than the other three and dealt with the increasing separation of and tensions between Jews and Christians.

During the next twenty centuries opinions about Jesus became even more diverse. He was portrayed as a peacemaker and a warrior, a martyr and a judge, a king and a shepherd. In the first three centuries of its history, Christianity was illegal and therefore had relatively little power and influence in the secular world. The government periodically persecuted Christians who refused to renounce their faith. During this period artists often portrayed Christ as the good shepherd who comforted suffering Christians. After the conversion of the emperor Constantine in 312 CE, Christianity became the accepted religion of the Roman Empire and gained enormous power and influence. Artists now portrayed Christ as a powerful king or judge. A fifth-century mosaic in a Roman church shows Christ seated on a throne, holding a sword and looking fierce and dangerous. When Christianity was weak and struggling, Christ was portrayed as a comforting presence who did not threaten the established political powers. When Christianity gained power, the image of Christ became more threatening, as if to compel belief. The perception of Jesus was shaped by cultural realities.

There has been a great deal of variety in the ways people understand and experience Jesus. In the early twentieth century Albert Schweitzer read a number of biographies of Jesus and concluded that each author's personality and interests helped to shape the Jesus he described. A life of Jesus said more about its author than about its subject.[1] Nearly a century later, it is not surprising that African American theologians consider the implications of Jesus' race and the meaning of a black Messiah, and that feminist theologians consider the implications of Jesus' gender. Jesus has been a powerful and influential symbol in Western culture, and various groups and individuals find that they need to discern his significance for their lives.

Despite all the diverse perspectives on Jesus, not everything was completely open to interpretation. Some distinctive claims about Jesus were made and often vigorously debated. For almost two thousand years most Christians agreed that Jesus was no ordinary human being. He was God's only begotten Son and the Word who "became flesh and lived among us" (John 3:16; 1:14). He possessed miraculous powers to heal and to cast out demons, and he also claimed the ability to forgive sins. He identified himself with God, even calling God his Father, which infuriated many of the Jewish people he encountered, who believed there was only one God. He also identified himself as the Messiah, or Christ, the anointed one who the prophets had promised would bring salvation to Israel. After he died on the cross he rose from the dead and later ascended into heaven to be with God. Several centuries later, in 325, the Council of Niaea tried to settle a fierce debate by affirming that Jesus was not a created being and not merely human, but of the same substance as God.

Christians also claimed that Jesus was fully human. Humanity was not a mask or a disguise that enabled a divine being to pretend to be human, but a reality. Jesus experienced hunger, thirst, exhaustion, and temptation. He differed from human beings only in his perfection. He was tempted, but never sinned. This mix of human and divine in Jesus, like his relationship with God, is not easy to fathom. In 451 the Council of Chalcedon attempted to resolve debate by affirming that Jesus was both fully human and fully divine.

Both of these doctrinal statements have been challenged, but during the past two centuries an increasing number of questions have been posed about the identity of Jesus. Can he be fully human if he is perfect and sinless? Can a divine figure be fully human if he continues to possess divine powers? A number of scholars have suggested that Jesus was a very good man who lived an exemplary life, but he was not divine. He may have been particularly aware of and connected to God, but he was not God himself. Some scholars question the divinity of Jesus because it seems irrational and impossible. Others suggest that if he really was divine he would have possessed more power and could have attacked the status quo more effectively than he did. Jacquelyn Grant asked, for example, "If Jesus was more than human—that is, also divine, why did he not miraculously or directly overthrow the evil powers which keep women in oppression?"[2]

Other Christians refuse to assert that Jesus is divine or unique because it leads to the assumption that Christianity is the only, or at least the best, way to encounter God. This claim has led to various forms of cultural and religious imperialism. The Crusaders in the eleventh and twelfth centuries believed that they were justified in murdering Muslims and destroying their property because they did not believe in the divinity of Jesus Christ. The Nazis and other groups throughout history offered a similar rationale for the murder of Jews. Missionaries preached Jesus Christ to the "heathen" or the "pagans," but did not respect the cultural and religious beliefs of the world's people. Carter Heyward concluded that "Christian faith and practice is necessarily destructive to most people in the world insofar as it is cemented in the insistence that Jesus Christ is Lord and Savior of all."[3]

If Jesus is simply another human being, though, why are his opinion and example so important? Why spend a chapter on Christology if he is simply one of us? Why debate the meaning of his maleness if Jesus was simply an ordinary human being? Why do his teachings matter twenty centuries later? Eleanor McLaughlin observed pointedly, "If Jesus is not something more than a first-century Jewish rabbi, this enterprise is more trouble than it is worth."[4] In the past two centuries Christian feminists and others have argued that Jesus was a very good person who models a relationship with God, inspires the development of community, and encourages people to resist the powers that enslave them. This claim poses the question of whether an ordinary human being has such powers. Certainly there are heroic martyr figures like Martin Luther King, Jr., who serves as a role model despite his human limitations. Or was Jesus unique, then and now, because he provides not only an example of a good life, but also the power to live it?

Was Jesus a Feminist? Biblical Perspectives on Jesus

A common Christian interpretation of Jesus and his relationship to women asserts that he called only men to be his disciples. He never ordained women or made any radical changes in the status of women. He spent far more time with men and regularly affirmed male leadership. If he had wanted women to have a different role in church and society, he certainly would have made a point of it. Jesus was nice to women, but he never expected them to be treated as equals in the church. Such a reading tends to support the status quo and traditional roles for women.

Others interpreters draw from the Bible a profoundly different picture of Jesus. In 1971 Leonard Swidler wrote an article entitled "Jesus was a Feminist"[5] in which he noted that Jesus cared for women and elevated their status by taking them seriously. He resisted patriarchal structures and traditional assumptions and clearly demonstrated his support for women. Other feminist biblical scholars have argued that the word *feminist* may be anachronistic when applied to Jesus, but they agree that he treated women well.

In a culture where men did not speak with women on a regular basis, Jesus held theological conversations with them. In a culture where men were not supposed to touch women, Jesus encountered a woman who had been bent over for eighteen years, touched her, and healed her (Luke 13:10-17). When a woman with a bleeding disease that made her ritually unclean touched his clothing (thereby making him unclean also), he was not offended, but praised her great faith (Mark 5:34).

In a culture where women were supposed to be silent and docile, Jesus encountered a foreign woman who talked back. She asked him to heal her daughter, but he refused, explaining that he had been sent to the Israelites. Her courageous and thought-provoking reply encouraged Jesus to change his mind and expand the scope of his ministry to the gentile world (Mark 7:24-30).

In a culture where women had little education and some religious leaders believed that it was blasphemous to teach sacred texts to women,

Jesus affirmed Mary of Bethany for her desire to study and learn, even when her sister Martha complained that Mary neglected her kitchen duties (Luke 10:38-42).

In a culture where women were not trusted to testify as witnesses, Jesus appeared to women after his resurrection and charged them to go and tell what they had seen. Though some of the disciples dismissed their words as an "idle tale," the Gospels assert that women first proclaimed the good news that Jesus Christ was risen (Matt 28:1-10; Luke 24:1-12). Earlier in his career Jesus encountered a Samaritan woman and asked her for a drink, even though that was against the religious and social customs of his time. After a theological conversation in which she recognized that he was the Messiah, she went and told her people about him, and "many believed in him because of the woman's testimony" (John 4:1-42).

In a culture where women were sometimes distrusted for their sexuality, Jesus related to women in an open, honest way. To the woman caught in adultery he simply said, "Go, and sin no more" (John 8:1-11 KJV). When a woman came uninvited to a dinner party and washed his feet with her tears and anointed his head with expensive ointment, he received her gifts without revulsion or discomfort (Mark 14:3-9).

The Gospels suggest that Jesus cared deeply about women and valued their contributions. He encouraged women to learn and to speak. He healed women, learned from them, and accepted their financial and emotional sustenance. He affirmed women as valuable and fully human, so it seems legitimate to conclude that he was and is a positive figure for women. Dorothy Sayers summarized this perspective in an essay written in 1947:

> Perhaps it is no wonder that the women were first at the Cradle and last at the Cross. They had never known a man like this Man— there never has been such another. A prophet and teacher who never nagged at them, never flattered or coaxed or patronized; who never made arch jokes about them, never treated them either as "The women, God help us!" or "The ladies, God bless them!"; who rebuked without querulousness and praised without condescension; who took their questions and arguments seriously; who never mapped out their sphere for them, never urged them to be feminine or jeered at them for being female; who had no axe to grind and no uneasy male dignity to defend; who took them as he found them and was completely unself-conscious. There is no act, no sermon, no parable in the whole Gospel that borrows its pungency from female perversity; nobody could possibly guess from the words and deeds of Jesus that there was anything "funny" about women's nature.[6]

If Jesus can be understood so positively, why is there a problem? He seems relatively egalitarian for his time. What's not to like? Feminist theologians have highlighted three problems that stem from the claim that Jesus was a feminist.

First, the fact that Jesus was nice to women does not mean that he actually challenged the structures of patriarchy and sexism. He supported Mary of Bethany, but he did not publicly affirm the right of all women to study and learn. He did not encourage men to share domestic work and child care in order to give women more freedom. He did not teach the importance of equality in a clear and unambiguous manner.[7] Jesus' kindness to women was not continued by the church, which has been ambivalent and even hostile toward them. Church leaders have argued that just because Jesus was nice to women does not mean he wanted them to be ordained or to hold leadership roles. Feminists wonder why Jesus did not have a more lasting influence on the church, which developed in his name. If Jesus really cared about women, why hasn't that concern been clear in the history of Christianity?

A second problem is whether a truly feminist Jesus would expect women to look up to, worship, and obey a male role model. Mary Daly argued that women do not need either biblical texts or role models from the past to justify their struggle for equality. In response to the claim that Jesus was a feminist, she said tartly, "Fine, great, but even if he wasn't, I am." She advised women to trust the validity of their own experience, not to imitate someone from a very different world.[8]

Other feminists argue that the problem is the *male* role model. Carter Heyward noted the expectation in Christianity that women "must constantly look up—for inspiration, leadership, role-modeling, and redemption—to a man."[9] Jesus is portrayed not only as a man, but also as a perfect, sinless, divine man. Can women live up to his example? Elisabeth Schüssler Fiorenza doubted that Jesus could be a role model for women, "since feminist psychological liberation means exactly the struggle of women to free themselves from all male internalized norms and models."[10]

Feminists have also questioned the *kind* of role model Jesus embodies—obedient, subordinate, submissive, suffering without complaint. Women have been taught all too well by the Christian tradition that although they do not resemble Jesus enough to be priests, they can imitate his sacrificial love, humility, meekness, and passive acceptance of suffering. Women do not need more encouragement to deny themselves and live for others, from Jesus or from any other model.

A third problem with the claim that Jesus is a feminist is that scholars sometimes justify their arguments by pointing out the perceived deficiencies of Judaism and the nasty way the Jews treated women. They then claim that Jesus repudiated the horribly legalistic, misogynist religious system in which he was reared. Jewish feminists have replied that these charges are inaccurate, and that it is unfair and anti-Semitic to portray Judaism as completely sexist while lifting up Jesus and Christianity as the great redeemers of women. Jesus was a Jew whose ethics, religious life, and relationship with God were significantly formed by the teachings and practices of Jewish law. During his ministry Jesus criticized the rigidities and excesses of religion, especially legalism and exclusivism; but he would probably be equally critical today of some of the rigidities of the Christian faith. He did not repudiate Judaism or create a new religion out of nothing. Christianity is deeply rooted in Judaism, and therefore Judaism cannot simply be dismissed as oppressive to women in order to make Christianity look more egalitarian.[11]

Was Jesus a feminist? The term may be anachronistic, but his affirmation of and relationships with women and his recognition of their full humanity suggests that he sought justice for women well before such an action was common.

Can a Male Savior Save Women?
The Meaning of Maleness

The most trenchant feminist criticism is not directed at the person of Jesus because, as the previous discussion suggests, he was generally supportive of women. The problem is the way his maleness has been misunderstood and misused to exclude women from the priesthood and from full equality. A common English translation of the Nicene Creed says that Jesus "became man for us men and for our salvation," which implies that the important theological issue was that Jesus became a man, particularly for the salvation of men. A more accurate translation of the Latin would say that he "became human for us and for our salvation." The question is not simply one of semantics or politically correct language, but of who is included in the salvation of God.

Gender was certainly part of Jesus' identity as a person, as it is for all human beings; however, the essential theological point of the Incarnation was not that he became a male, but that he became fully human. Theologians in the early church insisted that Jesus was not just pretending to be human, nor was he dressed in human flesh to disguise his divine nature. If he was not fully human, then the incarnation was a sham and he could not have been tempted as humans were. Jesus could only save human nature by taking it on and becoming one with it, or as one common way of putting the matter in the early church said, "Whatever is not assumed, is not redeemed." If Jesus had assumed only male nature, in a way that did not fully include female nature, it would be impossible for women to be saved. Clearly, that is not the case. Those Christians who insist that Jesus *had* to be a man and that maleness was somehow essential to the Incarnation may be treading on thin theological ice.

The maleness of Christ is also misused when the church claims that those who represent Christ must be male. Aquinas and others believed that although women could be redeemed by Christ, their female nature made them essentially different from him and therefore they could not represent him in the priesthood. The Vatican stated explicitly in 1976 that priests must bear a physical resemblance to Christ in order to represent him. Priests need not be young or Jewish, but they must be male. Rosemary Radford Ruether observed,

> Since this strange new version of the imitation of Christ does not exclude a Negro, a Chinese or a Dutchman from representing a first-century Jew, or a wealthy prelate from representing a carpenter's Son, or sinners from representing the saviour, we must assume this imitation of Christ has now been reduced to one essential element, namely, male sex.[12]

Early in the nineteenth century, Jarena Lee made a similar point to those who wanted to deny her the right to preach based on the maleness of Jesus. "If the man may preach, because the Saviour died for him, why not the woman? seeing he died for her also. Is he not a whole Saviour, instead of half one? as those who hold it wrong for a woman to preach, would seem to make it appear."[13]

Feminist theologians do not deny that Jesus was a man, as is sometimes assumed, but they refuse to use maleness in ways are theologically inappropriate. Elizabeth Johnson wrote:

> The fact that Jesus of Nazareth was a man is not in question. His maleness is constitutive for his personal identity, part of the perfection and limitation of his historical reality, and as such it is to be respected. His sex is as intrinsic to his historical person as are his race, class, ethnic heritage, culture, his Jewish religious faith, his Galilean village roots, and so forth. The difficulty arises, rather, from the way this one particularity of sex, unlike the other historical particularities, is interpreted in sexist theology and practice. Consciously or unconsciously, Jesus' maleness is lifted up

and made essential for his christic function and identity, thus blocking women precisely because of their female sex from participating in the fullness of their Christian identity as images of Christ.[14]

How should the maleness of Jesus be understood? Feminist theologians believe that the maleness of Christ was not essential to the Incarnation. God may well have had a good reason for taking on male flesh rather than female, but the reasons had more to do with the culture of the first century than with the meaning of the Incarnation or the gender of God. Maleness may have been a cultural necessity, but it was not a theological necessity.

Perhaps God chose maleness to make a point to both men and women. Elizabeth Johnson wrote: "If in a patriarchal culture a woman had preached compassionate love and enacted a style of authority that serves, she would most certainly have been greeted with a colossal shrug. Is this not what women are supposed to do by nature?"[15] Jesus was able to be a servant because he chose to be, not because he had to be. A male Jesus was able to challenge patriarchy and choose to live without the privileges of maleness in the same way that the human Jesus chose to live without divine powers. He chose to spend most of his time with the weak, the broken, the outcast. He chose to relate to people as a servant rather than as a ruler. He waited to be received rather than to force himself upon an unwilling world. He chose to be gentle and relational rather than harsh and domineering. Such a way of life is a powerful gift for both men and women, and as Johnson observed: "The heart of the problem is not that Jesus was a man but that too many men have not followed his footsteps, insofar as patriarchy has defined their self-identity and relationships."[16]

Could God have become incarnate in a woman? It would seem that an all-powerful God could have chosen to take female form and thereby overcome all the patriarchal assumptions and cultural obstacles. It would have made a profound statement to women if God had clearly affirmed women and femaleness. But just as the divine took on the limitations of the human, so God also chose to work within the limits of historical reality and human freedom. God came at a particular time and took on flesh as a particular person. God accommodated to human capacity, and one cannot be a human without having a particular gender. The choice of male gender, however, was not necessary because God was male or to make salvation effective or because female flesh was not worthy of God. A male savior can save women because the saving significance of Jesus is not his maleness, but his humanity.

Positive Models of Jesus

Feminist theologians have spent much time and energy criticizing erroneous interpretations of Jesus, but they have also made many creative contributions to revisioning the way he is understood. Many feminists theologians have found Jesus to be a positive and empowering person and symbol.

Liberator

The Gospels contain many stories in which Jesus liberates or sets a person free from the bondage of sin; physical or mental illness; or social, economic, or religious oppression. Like the prophets before him, he criticized the institutions that perpetuated poverty and human suffering and challenged them to change. Rosemary Radford Ruether wrote of this role: "His ability to be liberator does not reside in his maleness but, on the contrary, in the fact that he has renounced this system of domination and seeks to embody in his person the new humanity of service and mutual empowerment."[17]

Feminist theologians from the Third World also speak frequently about Jesus' ability to liberate from all the oppressions that affect women and men of different races and classes throughout the world.

> In the person and praxis of Jesus Christ, women of the three continents find the grounds of our liberation from all discrimination: sexual, racial, social, economic, political, and religious. . . . This means that Christology is integrally linked with action on behalf of social justice and the defense of each person's right to life and to a more humane life.[18]

Despite what they have sometimes been told about Jesus as primarily the Savior of their souls, these women have a vivid sense of Jesus as a very present help in trouble who does not sit unconcerned in heaven but participates in their struggle. He does not support the status quo and the oppression it often fosters, but actively worked in his own time, and works now, to liberate people from apartheid, racism, poverty, and exploitation.

It is possible that emphasizing the liberating work of Jesus could produce passivity and discourage human efforts for justice. If Jesus will fix everything or if transformation will not occur until heaven, then human beings have little role to play. Carter Heyward warned that women, black, poor, and gay and lesbian Christians participate in the perpetuation of our own oppression insofar as we allow our visions and energies to be drawn toward a heavenly man and away from our human situation as sisters and brothers, by fixing our attention on the spiritual accomplishments of a divine Savior rather than on the spiritual possibilities of a concerted human commitment that can be inspired by the Jesus story as a human story: a story of human faith, human love, and human possibility as the agency of divine movement in history.[19]

Jesus liberates the soul from sin, but his work does not end there. He liberates human beings from the oppressions that bind them and encourages, empowers, and enables their continued efforts for their own liberation and that of others.

Co-sufferer

What about those women whose liberation is incomplete and who continue to suffer from racism, sexism, and economic oppression? Many feminist theologians, especially from the Third World, find in Jesus' suffering, death, and resurrection a meaning for their own suffering. The suffering of Jesus gives them courage. A South African woman wrote, "There are times when I want to give up, but the pain that Christ went through gives me the strength to go on preaching the good news of a liberating God."[20]

Jacquelyn Grant and other womanist theologians also emphasize the role of Jesus as divine co-sufferer. In the midst of their experience of slavery, African American women developed the conviction that because Jesus had suffered unjustly he was particularly able to understand their unjust suffering and to give them comfort and strength. This vision of Jesus did not encourage passivity, as Grant observed:

> To affirm Jesus' solidarity with the "least of the people" is not an exercise in romanticized contentment with one's oppressed status in life. For as the Resurrection signified that there is more to life than the cross for Jesus Christ, for Black women it signifies that their tri-dimensional existence is not the end, but it merely represents the context in which a particular people struggle to experience hope and liberation.[21]

Korean women also spoke of the presence of Jesus in their suffering, emphasizing that he does not merely share their misery, but transforms it. They described their particular experience of suffering as *han,* a concept that unites their resentment and indignation about injustice with a deep sense of resignation, defeat, and powerlessness. Jesus not only offers healing and comfort, but also transforms the sense of defeat into an "energizing force for social change."[22] He chose to live in poverty and humility, and therefore is particularly able to be in solidarity with those who suffer and to give them strength and courage, not to passively accept their lives, but to survive and to resist.

Feminine imagery for Jesus

The final image of Jesus is drawn, not from contemporary feminist theology, but from the fourteenth century. Julian of Norwich described several ways in which Jesus Christ can be imaged as Mother. First, he gives birth to humanity through his death. "He carries us within him in love and travail, until the full time when he wanted to suffer the sharpest thorns and cruel pains that ever were or will be, and at the last he died." Jesus wanted to continue working in human lives, so he nourished them. "The mother can give her child to suck of her milk, but our precious Mother Jesus can feed us with himself, and does, most courteously and tenderly, with the blessed sacrament, which is the precious food of true life. . . . The mother can lay her child tenderly to her breast, but our tender Mother Jesus can lead us easily into his blessed breast through his sweet open side." Mothers then rear their children, changing their methods as appropriate to the age of the child. When children get in trouble they go to their mothers for help, and Jesus asks that human beings come to him in the same way. Julian wrote, "So he wants us to act as a meek child, saying: My kind Mother, my gracious Mother, my beloved Mother, have mercy on me. I have made myself filthy and unlike you, and I may not and cannot make it right except with your help and grace."[23]

This powerful imagery is not without its difficulties. To speak of Mother Jesus with male pronouns causes the same sort of disjuncture as did the "breasts of God the Father" in the discussion of God language. Linking the feminine so explicitly with maternal qualities has the potential to create limiting stereotypes of women as mothers and nothing else. Using maternal imagery to describe the suffering and sacrifice of Jesus may reinforce the notion that mothers should sacrifice everything for their children. Still, Julian's language is profound and provocative and offers an intriguing way to image the role of Jesus in human life.[24]

Does Maleness Matter?

Brian Wren reflected on his attempt to understand the questions feminist theologians have posed about the maleness of Jesus.

How would we feel about praying to a female Savior? What would it mean for us if a woman had been crucified for our sins? How would it feel to be taught, from boyhood, that God became Woman for the salvation of all women?. . . Asking myself these questions, I found a residual prejudice: the idea of God becoming incarnate in a woman startled me more than the idea of God becoming incarnate in a man. . . . I realize that if God's Anointed One was a woman, then however deeply saved and called I was by her life, death, and resurrection, I would always be aware that she was she and I was he. Her femaleness would highlight the differences between us and would be (potentially or actually) an obstacle to faith.[25]

Wren went on to describe a Jesus who challenged patriarchy and chose to live as a servant without the trappings of power. He chose to care for the poor and marginalized. He spent his ministry offering freedom, healing, forgiveness. He gave people courage. He listened and cared. He was a remarkable presence in his time and continues even now to enable, encourage, and heal. Wren wrote a hymn that summarizes this understanding of Jesus.

Great God, in Christ you call our name and then receive us as your own,
not through some merit, right or claim, but by your gracious love alone.
We strain to glimpse your mercy-seat and find you kneeling at our feet.
Then take the towel, and break the bread, and humble us, and call us friends.
Suffer and serve till all are fed and show how grandly love intends to work till all creation sings, to fill all worlds, to crown all things.
Great God, in Christ you set us free your life to live, your joy to share.
Give us your Spirit's liberty to turn from guilt and dull despair and offer all that faith can do while love is making all things new.[26]

The role of Jesus in human life and in the Christian tradition ultimately has little to do with maleness and everything to do with a love that is making all things new.

CHAPTER 6

Salvation

I n her novel *The Rapture of Canaan*, Sheri Reynolds tells the story of twelve-year-old Ninah Huff, a Southern girl who belonged to the Church of Fire and Brimstone and God's Almighty Baptizing Wind, a family church that her grandfather began and led. The church had a long list of rules and strict punishments for disobedience. Salvation came to those who knew their place, did as they were told, believed as Grandpa Herman did, and occasionally "got the spirit" and spoke in tongues.[1]

Salvation through obedience and correct belief has been a common theme in Christian tradition. The apostle Paul told his jailer to "Believe on the Lord Jesus, and you will be saved, you and your household" (Acts 16:31). Revivalists preach that people can be saved by coming forward, confessing their sins, and accepting Jesus into their hearts.

Other deeply religious people have recognized that their faith and good works have not been enough to save them from oppression. The psalmists repeatedly ask, "How long, O Lord?" How long will God leave them in despair and trouble before rescuing them? This cry has been heard from places such as South Africa or El Salvador where people are oppressed and enslaved because of their race or political opinions. In the movie *Romero* a young woman named Lucia told Archbishop Oscar Romero that her people in El Salvador needed to hear a message of hope from the church, because "it's so bad here." Lucia combined her faith in God with political activism against an oppressive government, as did Romero, and eventually both were murdered by those who wanted to preserve the government's power. They sought a salvation that would affect both the soul and the body.

American culture, on the other hand, offers a vision of salvation and the good life that emphasizes the body rather than the soul. Television commercials and news and fashion magazines illustrate the good life: Prozac, alcohol, cigars. Money, lots of money. A hot car. A thin, fit body. The latest self-help book. A cruise to an exotic island. The government promises salvation through the right welfare program, tax reform, or peace initiative. Pop psychology says that salvation comes from healing the inner child or becoming assertive.

Myths and fairy tales offer vivid images of salvation. Snow White awoke from her deathlike trance when the prince kissed her. The dying Beast was transformed back into a prince when Beauty (Belle) said she loved him. Simba found his vocation, his place in the circle of life. Pinocchio became a real boy. In fairy tales evil is punished or destroyed, truth and love win in the end, and the good people live happily ever after.

It seems to be part of the human condition to hope for things to be different and to pray for miracles. And things do change. Good things sometimes come from bad situations. Deeply wounded people do survive the horrible things that happen to them. People receive incredible surprises and undeserved gifts. They are loved and love in return. Such experiences of grace and goodness begin to illuminate the Christian doctrine of salvation.

Traditional and Biblical Views of Salvation

Many Christians believe that salvation rescues individuals from the consequences of sin and permits their souls to enter heaven when they die. The unsaved person is estranged from God. The saved person has a relationship with God that provides happiness and future security. Salvation affects the soul more than the body. It offers heavenly rewards to the individual, not earthly improvements to social structures. Salvation makes people right with God, but says little about right relationships within society.

The definition of salvation is closely linked to the definition of sin. If sin is a broken relationship between an individual and God, then the obvious solution is reconciliation, which occurs by repentance, conversion, "getting right with God," and developing a personal relationship with Christ. If sin is defying God through pride, self-seeking, and arrogance, then salvation requires a breaking of the self. Sinful people must recognize their weakness and failure, confess their need for God, and admit their inability to save themselves or their world. Salvation comes when the self is broken and gives up its own desires. Saved people will be self-sacrificing, unselfish, and not demand their own way.

The biblical understanding of salvation is actually much broader than this and includes the well-being of both individuals and society. The Hebrew Scriptures emphasized the salvation of a people or a nation. God made a covenant with Abraham and Sarah and promised they would be ancestors of a great nation. When the people of this nation became slaves in Egypt, God saved them and delivered them from oppression (Exod 14:30). God chose to save Israel in part so that individuals could develop relationships with God, but primarily so that Israel would be a light to the nations and a means by which God related to the whole world. God blessed Israel in order to bless all the nations (Gen 12:2-3).

Later in the Israelites' history, after they repeatedly broke their covenant with God and failed to live as God's people, the prophets called them back to right relationships. Religious faith meant not simply believing in and obeying God, but also doing justice for the neighbor and treating the stranger with compassion. When the Israelites were defeated in battle and exiled from their land, the prophets promised that in the future they would find shalom, or wholeness and peace, both as individuals and as a nation. Jeremiah 31:7-14, for example, contains many images of salvation. The scattered people will be gathered. They shall be radiant over the goodness of the Lord. Their life shall become like a watered garden. They will rejoice and be merry. Other biblical texts suggest that shalom will include economic equity, justice, and healing.

Similarly in the Gospels, Jesus made it clear that salvation affects every aspect of life. He forgave sins and invited people to repent and enter into a relationship with God; but he also healed physical diseases, cast out demons, cared for the poor and outcast, and challenged the religious and social customs of his time. He announced that in the kingdom of God the old rules about hierarchy, power, and wealth will be reversed. The meek will inherit the earth, and the poor will have a seat of honor at the banquet table. Salvation for Jesus involved wholeness, healing, and reconciliation for individuals and for society. He did not promise instant transformation, but the hope of the Kingdom and its radically new social structures.

Twenty years after the death and resurrection of Jesus, when it became clear that society had not yet been radically transformed, the apostle Paul tried to articulate the meaning of salvation for the early Christians. He introduced the concept of justification by faith and stressed the need for individual reconciliation with God. "God proves his love for us in that while we still were sinners Christ died for us. Much more surely then, now that we have been justified by his blood, will we be saved through him from the wrath of God" (Rom 5:8-9). Salvation for Paul meant that individuals are forgiven and offered new life and hope. When they encountered the grace of God, Christians would live responsibly with their neighbors and begin to break down the barriers that divided Jews and Gentiles, slaves and free, and men and women.

Later in the church's history, especially when it struggled against the powerful Roman Empire, salvation was often understood even more narrowly as the arrival of the soul into heaven after death. For Christians living with a government that sometimes killed them for their faith, this view was comforting and realistic, but it represented a major shift from the Israelite notion of shalom.

Despite the variety of images and the broad scope of salvation evident in the Bible, this individualistic, future-oriented view has dominated Christian thinking for most of its history. It allowed white slave owners to encourage slaves to be saved without questioning the legitimacy of slavery. It allowed wealthy businessmen to donate large sums of money to Christian institutions without paying their workers a living wage. It allowed the church fathers to pronounce that women could enter heaven, but not the pulpit. In response to this (mis)understanding of the tradition, feminist theologians have posed three questions.

Christian Feminist Critique of the Tradition

Can women be saved?

At first glance this seems like an outrageous question. Discussions about salvation in the Christian tradition usually emphasize that all men are sinful and need to be saved. The Nicene Creed affirms that Jesus became man "for us men and for our salvation." Are women included? They are usually assumed to be a subset of men, but in light of Christian beliefs that women are not fully human, that women are responsible for sin, and that Christ could not have been a woman, it is not outrageous but reasonable to wonder if salvation is fully effective for women or if they can be saved at all. Most Christians would insist that women can be saved, but a close look at their practices suggests that salvation may function differently for women. When men are forgiven and restored they become capable of ministry and service without restrictions, even though they continue to sin; but in some traditions women still have restrictions. Most of the Southern Baptist Convention refuses to ordain women because of Eve's sin. Salvation is apparently able to transform women sufficiently to keep them out of hell, but not enough to allow them a sacramental role at the altar. Salvation offers spiritual equality, but not equal roles.

Such arguments are rooted in Scripture, especially in 1 Timothy.[2] The

110

author instructed women to help others and to learn quietly, but not to teach or to tell men what to do. "After all, Adam was created before Eve, and the man Adam wasn't the one who was fooled. It was the woman Eve who was completely fooled and sinned" (1 Tim 2:13-14 CEV). Women's subordination is rooted in both creation and the Fall. Woman was created second, but sinned first, and her sin was worse than the man's. This suggests that the woman fell farther away from the created ideal than the man did and implies that the grace of God does not provide enough forgiveness to allow women positions of leadership and authority. This author was clearly not convinced that salvation completely freed women from the consequences of their sin.

The author raises additional questions for the contemporary reader when he concludes, "But women will be saved by having children, if they stay faithful, loving, holy, and modest" (CEV). He appears to contradict the Christian belief that salvation is a gift and grace of God, not something that is earned by good behavior. This passage also implies that childless women might be excluded from salvation.

Some interpreters of the text suggest that women continue their subordinate roles after redemption, not because divine forgiveness is insufficient, but because subordination was part of God's intention for creation. Redeemed women will never reach full equality with men because God established a hierarchy in which men graciously lead and women willingly submit. Salvation will help women submit graciously rather than reluctantly, but it will never remove the need to submit.[3]

Other readers have offered a more positive interpretation of the text. Thomas Oden suggested that the text offered some freedom to women because it permitted them to learn, which was rare in this cultural context. Women were not told to be silent, as some translators say, but attentive rather than arrogant. Oden suggested that the last verse could be translated, "The woman shall be saved through the Childbearing," meaning the birth of Jesus. Even if the woman was created second, and even if she was deceived, she could receive salvation from the birth of Christ.[4]

Feminist biblical scholars have noted that this text contradicts Paul's claims in Galatians 3:28 about equality and freedom in Christ. If salvation does not make women equal to men in all aspects of the Christian faith, it fails to be a source of empowerment and comfort for women and therefore is not real salvation. This text also contradicts biblical evidence that women were teaching and exercising leadership in the early church.[5]

In addition to asking what salvation means for women's roles in church and society, feminist theologians point to some troubling

Christian assumptions about salvation and the body. Throughout much of Christian history the future hope of heaven included the belief that people would be transformed into spiritual beings whose souls were freed from the limitations of the body. In heaven there would be no hunger, exhaustion, grief or pain, but also no sexual desire, sexual activity, or childbirth. For women, who were primarily defined by motherhood, salvation therefore meant the repudiation of their nature. Men would no longer be sexual beings either, but since men were not defined solely in terms of body and fatherhood, salvation for men did not repudiate, but perfected, their essential nature. Men became fully themselves, while women had to become more like men. Some of the church fathers described the ideal spiritual woman as one who renounced sexuality and motherhood and completely ignored her appearance, denying herself food, sleep, and baths.[6]

In this context it is not surprising that Mary Daly wrote in *Beyond God the Father*, "The beginning of liberation comes when women refuse to be 'good' and/or 'healthy' by prevailing standards. To be female is to be deviant by definition in the prevailing culture. To be female and defiant is to be intolerably deviant."[7] Salvation defined as submission, obedience, and repudiation of the female body does not seem like a liberating gift for women. When Promise Keepers encourages hierarchical relationships as the cure for troubled families and society, it is no wonder that feminists are skeptical of this definition of salvation.

Does salvation require a shattering of the self?

Salvation has often been understood in the Christian tradition as self-denial, or saying no to the self in order to obey God. If sin is defined as pride or overvaluing the self, then salvation requires the denial of self-interest, or as Reinhold Niebuhr put it, a shattering of the self. But if pride is not the besetting sin for women, they will not find grace and transformation in the demand that they give up even more of themselves. If teenage girls have already lost self-esteem and feel they must preserve relationships at the expense of stating their own opinions,[8] it will not be helpful for them to hear the church assert that pride and self-confidence are sins or that salvation can be found in giving up the self and its desires. Judith Plaskow wrote, "The shattering of the self from beyond is received as grace only where the self's sin is pride and self-absorption. Where sin is not 'too much' self but lack of self, such a shattering is at least irrelevant and possibly destructive rather than healing."[9] Self-sacrifice may be a helpful antidote to excessive self-seeking and self-assertion, but self-sacrifice can only be useful if there is a self to sacrifice.

Along with advice to give up the self and all its desires, women have been told they can achieve salvation through service to others. Women can achieve joy, they are told, by serving first Jesus, then others, then themselves. Women can counter their tendencies to pride and self-seeking and demonstrate their Christian commitment by putting the husband's job, the children's happiness, or the needs of the church ahead of their own needs. Roberta Bondi reflected on her childhood experience of watching her mother.

> Real women were supposed to suffer on behalf of their husbands and children, and this suffering was called "sacrifice." If the mother was exhausted with a new baby and the baby cried in the night, it was mama who got up because daddy needed his sleep. If there were two pieces of chicken and three family members, mother smilingly went hungry. . . . In the forties and fifties this behavior was expected of all mothers, not just mine. A woman's sacrifices proved to her husband and children that she loved them, and to the world that she was a good woman. They were the foundation of her moral authority in her family; without them she could never hope to win the guilty gratitude of her children and her husband.[10]

The experience of women may have improved in the last four decades, and there may be a bit less emphasis on maternal sacrifice. Certainly women have more options now. The debate about working mothers, however, suggests that women are still expected to sacrifice for their children. Working women who want to "have it all" are labeled selfish and uncaring. Working fathers who occasionally volunteer in the classroom are heroes. Perhaps salvation for women is found, not in eradicating the desire to have it all, but in transforming social structures in such a way that working and parenting are not mutually exclusive.

Salvation for women has often meant being quiet and submissive, not angry or self-assertive. Daphne Hampson argued that salvation for women includes learning to take themselves seriously as persons with needs and rights. This is not being selfish or denying the rights of others, but realizing that women need to care for and value themselves.[11] Similarly, womanist theologians insist that salvation for African American women comes, not through humility and service, but by elevating and healing their self-esteem.[12]

Feminist theologians believe that people struggle with different forms and degrees of sin and therefore find salvation and healing in different remedies. To tell insecure and frightened people that pride is sinful will not help them develop into the people God intended them to be. The meaning of salvation will vary for people depending on the nature of the sin that haunts them.

Can oppressive structures be saved?

Liberation theologians, black, feminist, Hispanic, and Asian, argue that if evidence of sin can be found in oppressive social structures and institutions, salvation should enable at least the beginning of their transformation. If racism and sexism and other injustices are sins, then salvation should begin to dismantle these damaging forms of human behavior. The church and individual Christians should speak out and take action against poverty, oppression, and injustice.

For much of its history, however, the church has been cautious and relatively silent about salvation for social structures. The church has claimed that social structures cannot be converted and that only transformed individuals can transform society. Christians have argued that a vision of salvation that includes human rights and equality is secular rather than religious and that the church ought to concentrate on its primary task, the saving of souls. Some Christians attributed poverty and slavery to the will of God, who desired an ordered, hierarchical society. When slaves, women, and the poor protested that oppression was inconsistent with the Christian faith, the church replied that the gospel only promised spiritual equality. Salvation did not guarantee wealth for the poor or freedom for slaves, but only a space in heaven for their souls. Those who suffered injustice on earth should not fight back, but await their heavenly reward. It was selfish to expect more.

Feminist and liberation theologians argue that a biblical doctrine of salvation must deal with the transformation of structures and systems as well as of individuals. The vision of a new and improved future comes, not from secular values, but from Scripture. The prophets envision a future when both human beings and the whole creation can become what they were created to be and live in harmony. Joel Tanis, an artist who illustrates biblical texts from a child's point of view, offered this interpretation of Isaiah 11:6-9 on one of his prints:

> The Bible says some day the wolf will live with the lam, or maybe the 3 little pigs, plus lions and tiggers and bares will live with cows and baby cows (cafs) and nice animals like rabbits. Insted of eating the fluffy little animals, the big mean animals will eat straw. And the hole world will be happy. Speshully the fluffy little animals.

Paul wrote that the whole creation waits to be set free from its bondage. (Rom 8:19-23). Other biblical texts show God taking the side of those who are mistreated or demeaned, often with some harsh words for those who oppress others. Liberation theologians believe that if shalom in the Old Testament and the Kingdom in the New Testament included justice for

114

the oppressed, contemporary Christians' notions of salvation should do the same. Social transformation may be slow, difficult, and not fully realizable in this world, but it is worth the effort. God's grace comes to structures as well as to people in the hope that the social order will continue to develop into a place of justice and freedom for all God's people.

"All Will Be Well": Feminist Perspectives on Salvation

The feminist critique has named the weaknesses of the traditional Christian doctrine of salvation, but feminist theology also offers a positive vision of the meaning of salvation in human lives. Salvation affects three dimensions of life: the individual's relationship with God, the individual's relationship with other people and with the world, and the individual's sense of the self.

Julian of Norwich, the fourteenth-century mystic, summarized her understanding of salvation with the phrase, "All will be well, and all manner of things will be well." She emphasized God's constant grace, mercy, and love and God's compassionate desire to restore the world. God cares deeply about the world and wishes, not to punish, but to heal it. She described the surprising mixture in human beings of goodness and sin, despair and hope. "It certainly is a marvellous mix up! But the one thing that matters is that we always say 'Yes' to God whenever we experience him, and really do will to be with him, with all our heart and soul and strength."[13]

"All will be well" means that one's relationship with God is transformed. It means saying yes to God, not because God is a tyrant who demands assent and requires obedience, but freely choosing to say yes and to enter into a relationship of joy and delight. At the beginning of *The Color Purple,* Celie saw God as a distant and uncaring old white man. Later she learned to think of God in the color purple and to respond to a God who wants to be appreciated. Saying yes to God means trusting a God who deeply loves human beings. It means saying yes to hope when despair is easier and more obvious. It means saying yes to forgiveness and transformation. It means saying yes to sharing God's priorities and concerns for the world. Salvation is not restrictive and binding, but a process of freedom and liberation. Salvation is less a breaking down of sin and pride and more a building up of a relationship with God. Salvation is not obeying rules, but being set free for relationship with God and others. Salvation enables a relationship with God based, not on fear, but on delight.

Salvation also means that all will be well in one's relationships. Reconciliation is not easy or instantaneous, but salvation enables the beginning of healing. Sometimes salvation provides the courage to break out of hurtful relationships. Sometimes it means the courage to confront in order to transform a relationship. Sometimes it means the ability to forgive someone and begin again. As a young woman Celie was married without her consent to a man she called "Mister." He needed a mother for his boys, and Celie's stepfather wanted to be rid of her. Mister's cruelty reaffirmed Celie's sense that she was worthless. However, at the end of the novel, despite all the pain he had caused her, they had developed a relationship of mutual love and affection, although they were no longer married. Transformation in *The Color Purple* involved the healing of relationships.

Salvation also transforms one's sense of self. Traditional Christian language speaks of forgiveness or conversion. Broken people find healing. Lost people find a sense of direction or vocation. Silenced people find a voice. One of the most powerful biblical stories of transformation occurs in the Gospel of Luke. A woman had been crippled for eighteen years with a disease that made her unable to stand up straight. Jesus met her in the synagogue one Sabbath, touched her, and announced that she was freed from her ailment. Some of the observers criticized him for healing on the sabbath, and others were offended because he touched a woman. Jesus, however, demanded of them whether she, as a daughter of Abraham, should not be freed from her bondage. He did not care that he broke the religious rules of the time because it was more important that this woman find healing and liberation. Her illness symbolizes the oppression and limitations that keep women all bent out of shape. Salvation meant freedom, healing, liberation, and standing up straight (Luke 13:10-17).

Salvation can mean finding one's vocation or calling. Celie began to make pants and found both financial security and the affirmation of her creativity and ability. Ninah Huff began weaving rugs. Vocation is a way that we give back to God and the world, not because we must, but because we want to share what we have with others.

Salvation can include finding a sense of joy and delight in one's life. Experiencing God's grace can be profoundly liberating as one is freed from the expectations of others to become the person one is meant to be. Some women find in the grace of God the assurance that they will survive even the most difficult experiences. Mary Pellauer told the story of an incest survivor. "She talked about going down into the abyss, further and further down until she touched bottom, and the bottom *held her up*."[14] Grace helps people to survive, and to thrive.

Ninah Huff's baby son, Canaan, was born with his hands held together by a piece of skin. The community decided that he was the new

Messiah because he looked like he was praying. Ninah noticed that he could not walk or play like other toddlers, and finally, in the midst of her own sense of alienation and frustration with the community, she cut his hands apart. After his initial tears and some spattering of blood, he began to squeal with delight. Ninah recalled an earlier incident when Corinthian, a dangerous outsider, had used the phrase "Whee, Jesus" and Ninah thought it was a curse. Now she remembered the words again. "But it wasn't a curse at all. It was a prayer, and not a frightened one. It was a prayer praising freedom."[15] Salvation can be like that—an experience of transformation and freedom so delightful that one responds, "Whee, Jesus."

These three phrases, "All will be well," "Whee, Jesus," and "saying yes to God," provide images of the wholeness, healing, and shalom that are part of the biblical understanding of salvation. Christian feminists believe that God wants men and women to be people of integrity, wisdom, passion, and compassion. God wants human beings to use the gifts God has given them to make a difference in the world. God provides the grace to help people turn from restricted, burdened, limited lives to discover the freedom God provides. God's salvation helps people to stand up straight; break free of the rules and expectations that bind them; and live freely, responsibly, and joyfully in the world God has made.

How does salvation happen? The meaning of the cross and the death of Jesus

Salvation seems like a wonderful gift that everyone would love to receive. But as with those envelopes that promise "You may have already won," we wonder what the catch might be. What must be done to receive this salvation? In the Christian tradition the catch, or the price for salvation, is the death of Jesus on the cross, or in formal terms, the atonement.

The doctrine of atonement in the Christian tradition is difficult, intellectually challenging, and mysterious. It asserts that the relationship between God and humanity has been broken because of sin. God is angry with human sinfulness and needs to punish it. In order for God and humanity to be reconciled or made "at one" something must happen so that God is no longer offended by sin. Theologians have developed complex theories to explain how salvation happens through the death of Jesus on the cross.

In the Old Testament, as in other religious traditions, reconciliation with God could occur through animal sacrifice. In a commentary on Leviticus Judith Romney Wegner described the importance of cosmic harmony and order in the Israelite worldview. If harmony was disturbed, a symbolic action was required to counteract the disturbance and restore order.[16] Anyone who offended God needed to placate God by offering an animal sacrifice. The animal took the punishment that the sinful person deserved, and the shedding of its blood was thought to have cleansing power. Sacrifices were not superstition, but symbolized a deep commitment to the ways of God and to the well-being of the community. They demonstrated repentance, gratitude to God, and a desire to live in God's way.

The New Testament adopts similar language of sacrifice and substitution to interpret the death of Jesus on the cross. The Gospels describe the event rather than explain it. Jesus caused conflict with religious and political leaders because he claimed to be the Messiah and he challenged the religious system. He so angered those in power that they killed him. Jesus believed that death would inevitably result from the way he chose to live. He predicted his suffering and death (Mark 8:31; 9:31) and said that the purpose of his life was not to be served, but to serve and to give his life a ransom for many (Mark 10:45). Christian tradition has claimed that his death was God's will. The Gospels relate that before the crucifixion Jesus prayed that he would not have to suffer, but nevertheless asked that God's will be done.

Two decades later the apostle Paul tried to make theological sense of the cross, particularly in his letter to the Romans. Christ sacrificed his life for human sin, Paul wrote, even though he was not sinful himself. Christ's death saved sinful human beings from God's wrath and reconciled them to God. He took on the death all humans deserved because of their sin. An exchange occurred. Jesus took on human sin, which he did not deserve; and human beings took on his righteousness, which they did not deserve.

In the centuries since Paul many theologians have wrestled with the meaning of the cross. Some suggested that the cross was a ransom paid to the devil to free humankind from the clutches of evil. Others said that the cross tricked the devil into believing that he was destroying Jesus, but Jesus ultimately destroyed him. These theories assume the presence of a devil or a Satanic figure who literally does battle with God and Jesus.

In the eleventh century Anselm explained the atonement in the categories of his culture. If the lord of a fiefdom was challenged by a disobedient subject, the lord must demand satisfaction or restitution. Similarly, human sin insulted God's honor. God demanded satisfaction, but sinful humans were unable to provide satisfaction. Since humans had committed the sin, only a human could satisfy it. Only a perfect person could satisfy God's honor, but there were no perfect persons. Finally God resolved the dilemma by sending Jesus Christ to live as a perfect human who would be able to offer satisfaction. This has been called the satisfaction theory of the atonement.

Several decades later, Abelard, a teacher and theologian, dismissed Anselm's explanation of the atonement as excessively legalistic. He argued that the cross illustrates the power of God's love and that Jesus saves people by showing them the depth of God's love for them and the way to live in response to God. This has been called the moral influence theory of the atonement.

These examples illustrate the variety of atonement theories in the Christian tradition. Theologians in different periods have explained the same event quite differently. Each theory says something true about the atonement, but no one adequately explains its mystery. The theories are often used in combination, as demonstrated in this hymn about the death of Jesus.

> Alas! and did my Savior bleed, and did my Sovereign die?
> Would he devote that sacred head for sinners such as I?
>
> Was it for crimes that I have done, he groaned upon the tree?
> Amazing pity! Grace unknown! And love beyond degree!
>
> But drops of tears can ne'er repay the debt of love I owe.
> Here, Lord, I give myself away; 'tis all that I can do.
>
> "Alas! and Did My Savior Bleed"
> Isaac Watts, 1707

Christian beliefs about the atonement emphasize the great chasm between a perfect God and "sinners such as I." Only God can reach across the chasm to sinful humanity, which God did in Jesus, the perfect human being. He became the scapegoat, in Old Testament language, who bore the sins of the whole community. Jesus died because it was the only way God could both punish sin and forgive it. The cross is the central symbol of the Christian faith because through it death was defeated and sin was forgiven. The resurrection then made possible new life for Jesus and for all humanity.

The Christian tradition does not claim that this is easy to understand or believe. Paul wrote in 1 Corinthians that the cross appears to many people as foolishness and a stumbling block because it does not make logical sense and offends human sensibilities in many ways. The difficulty of believing this seems to make it all the more essential.

Feminist critique of atonement theories

In a speech given in 1993 Delores Williams, a womanist theologian and professor at Union Theological Seminary, called feminist theologians to rethink the meaning of the cross. She proposed that the offensive images of dripping blood and a person hanging from a cross would not be necessary if people understood the importance of the life of Jesus. Her remarks sparked protest and controversy in many Protestant denominations. If the cross is unnecessary, critics asked, what becomes of Christianity? Do people no longer need God or Christ? Can they save themselves? Might salvation be obtained in ways other than the death of Jesus? Many Christians believe that the cross is essential to the Christian faith and therefore cannot be debated or critiqued.

Christian feminists agree that the cross is a powerful symbol, but find that it is sometimes destructive rather than helpful. They have articulated a number of questions about the doctrine of atonement, most of which can be categorized into three specific issues: God's nature, human nature, and the role of suffering.

First, what do the theories of atonement imply about the nature and character of God? A God who demands the sacrifice of an innocent man for the sins of humanity seems bloodthirsty, vengeful, and mean. If God is as gracious as Scripture sometimes suggests, it is possible that God could choose to forgive sin without bloodshed. Why would a loving father force his Son to die? How could any decent being force another to die?

Some feminist theologians suggest that this represents abusive behavior or "cosmic child abuse." Joanne Carlson Brown and Rebecca Parker said bluntly, "To argue that salvation can only come through the cross is to make God a divine sadist and a divine child abuser."[17] A God who responds so angrily and vindictively to human failure that he engineers the death of an innocent man does not seem like a God who invites relationship. Nancy Mairs labeled this being the "God of Gotcha" and observed, "It is awfully hard to achieve spiritual health in relation to a being who appears eager to condemn you so that he can then magnanimously redeem you from your own nasty nature."[18]

Perhaps God does not care so much about honor as the tradition has claimed. Some biblical stories show that God may simply choose to forgive without exacting a price. Jesus told a story in Luke 15 in which a son took his inheritance, left home, squandered all his money, then returned in disgrace, hoping his father would hire him as a servant. The father, who according to custom should have been deeply offended by the son's behavior, saw the son coming from a distance and ran to meet him. The father did not demand an apology or ask for satisfaction, but lavished his son with gifts. In the prophets God is at times angered by the people's rejection, but God's anger does not have the last word. Love and compassion win out in the end, and God chooses to be gracious even to people who disobey and resist.

Feminist theologians argue that the death of Jesus was not required by God as a payment for sin, but was a sinful act of violence perpetrated by human beings. Rita Nakashima Brock wrote, "Jesus' death was tragic, but it neither had to happen nor was part of a divine plan for salvation."[19] Jesus died, not because God demanded it as the price of reconciliation between God and humanity, but because his radical life threatened the religious and political powers of his time. His death was not God's choice, and it was not required to "clean the slate" and thereby enable God to love and accept sinful human beings.

Second, feminist theologians observe that these theories of atonement imply that human beings are so depraved that God can only accept them if someone dies for them. Human beings seem to be in an impossible situation because they are not good enough to relate to God, and yet they are punished for their inability. God demands perfection that humans are unable to produce.

Feminist theologians (as have other Christians before them) question the logic of the atonement. How can one person's death save another? How can one person's sin or goodness be transmitted to another? How could the death of Jesus change God's view of the rest of humankind? If a person guilty of murder was sentenced to the electric chair, he might find someone willing to die for him; but he would not be any less guilty because of the substitute.

The doctrine of the atonement also seems to promote passivity. Human beings can do nothing except wait for God to take the initiative. This may be a useful antidote to an egotistical desire to be the center of everything, but it does not seem very helpful to those women who need encouragement to act. Brock noted:

> We are not called to place our faith in benignly paternalistic powers who will rescue us or protect us from suffering. We are to have faith in our own worth, which empowers us to be healed by each other. . . . No one heroic or divine deed will defeat oppressive powers and death-delivering systems. We cannot rely on one past event to save our future. No almighty power will deliver us from evil. With each minute we wait for such rescue, more die.[20]

Brock believed that the power to heal brokenness comes from the strength of the community and from the individual's powers of courage and resistance. These internal and communal strengths are far more valuable than asking women to look to a man for salvation. Why does it take a man to make them right with God? Such encouragement of dependence is not helpful to women.

Third, Christian feminists have questioned the assumption that suffering and sacrifice are necessary for salvation. At times it appears that the Christian tradition glorifies suffering as the way to new life. Suffering as a prerequisite to love seems a sadistic contradiction to the notion of a God who loves freely. The belief that suffering can be redemptive is often applied to human life. Christians, especially women, are told that Jesus' suffering was redemptive and that their suffering can be also. In their essay on atonement theories, Brown and Parker wrote:

> The central image of Christ on the cross as the savior of the world communicates the message that suffering is redemptive. If the best person who ever lived gave his life for others, then, to be of value we should likewise sacrifice ourselves. Any sense that we have a right to care for our own needs is in conflict with being a faithful follower of Jesus. Our suffering for others will save the world.[21]

For example, some battered women have been told that Jesus suffered without complaint and that they should "turn the other cheek" just as he did.

The Christian tradition has not demanded that people die for the sins of others, but there is an influential strand in Christian thinking that encourages suffering. The letter to the Ephesians includes this instruction, "Husbands, love your wives, just as Christ loved the church and gave himself up for her" (Eph 5:25). In the early church Christians were promised heavenly rewards if they chose to die rather than renounce the faith. In the twentieth century Maria Goretti, a young Catholic girl, fought off a rapist who eventually murdered, but did not rape her. She was considered a saint because she gave up her life to protect her virginity. Various biblical texts and contemporary sermons challenge Christians to give up money, pleasure, happiness, success, or love to prove their faith, promising that good will result from their sacrifice. Women have been told to give up their careers, interests, and needs to better serve husband and children.

The advocates of traditional doctrine claim that the cross was a one-time event in which Jesus died for human sin. The cross cannot be repeated and was not meant to encourage martyrdom. Christian feminists respond that each variation of the atonement theory asks Christians to imitate the suffering of Christ, and it is this continual emphasis on self-sacrifice that makes the cross a dangerous and troubling symbol for women.

Feminist Revisioning of the Atonement Doctrine

Jesus as model

Some feminist theologians interpret the cross by emphasizing that the life of Jesus was more important than his death. Jesus had such a profound consciousness of God that he effectively listened to God and lived God's will. He showed others what it means to be fully human and connected to God. Human beings can move toward wholeness by following the teaching and example of Jesus. The cross is not necessary to restore the divine-human relationship.

Delores Williams pointed out that the Gospels, especially Luke 4:18, describe Jesus' ministry in terms of healing, casting out demons, preaching the good news, and showing compassion. He showed people how to live in peaceful, productive relationships with God and each other by demonstrating the power of faith and prayer. He provided a new vision of God, and he helped people to discover their vocations and deal with their limitations. Jesus did conquer sin, not as a substitute on the cross, but by the choices he made in his life. He resisted temptation in the wilderness. He refused to allow evil forces to have power over him. Redemption occurred through this ministerial vision. Williams concluded, "There is nothing divine in the blood of the cross. . . . Jesus came for life, to show humans a perfect vision of ministerial relation that humans had very little knowledge of. As Christians, black women cannot forget the cross, but neither can they glorify it. To do so is to glorify suffering and to render their exploitation sacred."[22] The life of Jesus was the most important part of his ministry, and Christians should imitate his life, not his suffering and death.

The cross as a sign of solidarity with human suffering.

Other feminist theologians insist that the cross does not symbolize divine anger and punishment, but God's concern for human suffering. Jesus died because he cared so deeply about the poor and the marginalized. He ate with prostitutes and tax collectors, he talked with and touched women, he sought justice for the oppressed. The world did not appreciate the way he challenged the powerful and inverted their value systems with claims that the meek would inherit the earth. Ellen Wondra concluded, "Jesus' own suffering and death are the outcome of a just life lived in resistance to an unjust world. They are a pouring out of self for the sake of others, consistent with the model of serving leadership given in his life."[23]

Perhaps because of their own experiences with political, economic, and racial suffering, feminist theologians from the Third World speak more positively about the cross and the atonement. Therese Souga wrote, "If Jesus is the God who has become weakness in our context, in his identity as God-man, Jesus takes on the condition of the African woman. The African woman can tell herself: Christ has been concerned with, and has been touched by, the situation that I am living."[24] Jesus took on and shared human suffering. Jesus became weak, but did not remain in that weakened state. He defeated death and thereby gives hope to others who suffer that one day their weakness and struggle will be transformed into new life.

Joanne Carlson Brown and Rebecca Parker found absolutely no redeeming value in suffering, even if it was freely chosen; but other feminists suggest that suffering for a purpose might have a positive result. During the Civil Rights movement in the United States and the efforts for economic justice in Central America, many people chose to suffer violence or jail time because they believed it would soften the hearts of the oppressors and achieve their desired goal. Jesus modeled this belief that "only suffering love has any chance of changing hearts."[25] Virginia Fabella wrote, "Like Jesus' suffering, women's active suffering has salvific value, for from the perspective of faith, every suffering, whether personally or vicariously experienced for the sake of building a more just world, falls within the ambit of salvation history."[26] These authors are careful not to bless suffering as God's will or to excuse the oppressive systems that often cause suffering, but they believe that God can bring something good out of pain and suffering.

Feminist theologians also argue that Jesus did not die because God forced him to or even because he had to under the terms of a divine plan. Letty Russell believed that Jesus chose to be for others and to be so fully human that he even experienced death. "It is Christ who performed the *first free act* in giving his life *for* many. The freedom of Adam and Eve *from* God and over against each other is a symbol of the old humanity. The new humanity is the beginning of a life that is for God and for others."[27] Choosing to be for others is very different from expected or enforced self-sacrifice. Choosing to be for others does not mean giving up the self completely for the sake of others. It is not obligation, but vocation, a choice to use one's abilities to care for and empower others, realizing that at times this choice results in suffering.

Death does not have the last word

Sally Purvis, in her book *The Power of the Cross*, suggested that the cross was not a sign of God's power, control, or anger over sin. The cross was not God's will or God's punishment for sin. God is not an abusive father defending his honor by demanding the death of his Son. Instead, the cross is a sign of God's vulnerability. When people did their worst, when grace and goodness had no effect, when death and destruction seemed to win, this was not the last word. An innocent man died on the cross because he cared for society's rejects and challenged society's treasured assumptions. God loved humanity so much that God was willing to be vulnerable, powerless, and weak; willing to let the powers of death do their work; and willing to be completely out of control. Purvis redefined the meaning of God's power.

> The power of God in the cross is not the power to die but the power to live. It is power that does not try to control events to affect one's will but rather power that brings forth life even from the desolation of defeat and death. The power of the cross is not the crucifixion but the resurrection—surprising, astonishing, utterly unpredictable.[28]

Life came from death because the power of love and life proved to be stronger than death. "Violence did its worst, and love and life went on."[29]

God's power is not controlling or violent and will not return evil for evil. "The cross shows God not in armed combat with the forces of evil, as so much Christian imagery would have it, but rather it shows God quietly, deeply, almost imperceptibly changing the terms of the conflict." The power of love wins in the end, not because it is physically stronger or more intimidating, but because it is God's way.[30]

Finally, Purvis challenged her readers, "Can we tolerate the cross as an authority for feminist Christian community? . . . can we learn to trust the cross, trust that it will not hurt us but will affirm and support our lives and loves?" She believed that feminists could trust the cross as a source of affirmation and support because the cross neither justified nor denied suffering. Suffering and pain exist for human beings, and God shared them on the cross. "The cross says very little to us about 'why'— why violence, why pain and suffering, why lack of control, why so much love? It simply stands as a witness to these realities, which cannot be explained but can be lived."[31]

The cross did not have the last word. God's love was stronger than death. The resurrection showed that death did not win and Jesus was not abandoned on the cross. The resurrection gives hope to all those who suffer, reminding them that God's love is stronger than the powers of death. A Palestinian woman spoke of resistance to the Israeli government and insisted that no amount of oppression would make her people give up their fight. "We are not helpless, and it is not hopeless. Isn't this also the message of the resurrection?"[32]

The cross as mystery

Reformed theologian Leanne Van Dyk pointed out that theories of atonement deal with a mystery. They do not completely define the workings of salvation and were not intended to.

> Rather, they suggest images of how salvation is effective. They seek to express in limited, analogical language the reality of God's decisive act on behalf of a broken world. There was some kind of victory that took place, some kind of power shift in the universe, some kind of ransom paid, some kind of healing initiated, some ultimate kind of love displayed, some kind of dramatic rescue effected. Of course, the terrible paradox of the Christian faith is that this rescue, this victory, this healing happened because of a death—a notorious, public execution. This is the dark mystery of the atonement. No theory of atonement can effectively account for that central paradox. Rather, the range of theories attempts to focus our attention, illuminate the truth, and point beyond themselves to God."[33]

The cross also demonstrates that salvation is not easy, cheap, or superficial. It is not simply riding off to the palace and living happily ever after, as in the fairy tales. "All will be well" is not a mantra that can be recited to promote positive thinking. The cross recognizes that there is much evil and brokenness, both in structures and in individuals, from which we need to be saved. And evil is persistent. Racism and sexism are very difficult to eradicate; and it is no easier to transform individual temptations to lust, greed, and manipulation or the propensity to think too highly of ourselves or not highly enough. The depth of such sinfulness must be taken seriously.

The cross and the broader vision of salvation confirm that there is a second reality in addition to that of sinfulness. Grace happens. Healing, transformation, and reconciliation occur. Christ is making all things new. All will be well. Sometimes grace occurs in almost miraculous ways. At other times goodness and mercy come in the form of other people or from internal resources that were previously unknown or unused. Grace sometimes comes in church; but it can be found in all places, even the most unlikely: the battlefield, the homeless shelter, the hospice unit. Grace sometimes comes to those who ask for it and sometimes to those who resist it. Grace enables the survival of one's own pain; the deep sympathy with another's pain; and, when appropriate, the joyful "Whee, Jesus." Salvation and the cross do not finally encourage passivity, but an openness to God and to each other, so that we can be both recipients and ministers of the goodness and mercy of God.

126

CHAPTER 7

Church and Ministry

On a winter day in the 1860s, Margaret Van Cott, a business-woman in New York City, stopped at a church to attend its noon prayer meeting.

About forty gentlemen were present, and she the only lady. The prayers were glorious, the testimony grand, and her heart began to feel the glow of Jesus' love. Five minutes before one o'clock she arose, and occupied three minutes testifying of the power of Christ to save. She was sweetly blest. The meeting closed, and as they descended the stairs, she was met by one, who, after considerable clearing of his throat, and a polite bow, said, "Ah, madam, ah—we—do not—ahem——"

Quick as thought the truth flashed through her mind that she was a woman, and had dared to speak of her precious Savior in the presence of men. She caught his words, and continued them, "You do not permit ladies to speak in your meetings."

"I won't say permit," was the reply, "but it is strictly a men's meeting; and there are plenty of places elsewhere where women can speak."

"I am aware of it, sir, thank God; but I thought I felt the Spirit of the Lord, and I am taught that 'where the Spirit of the Lord is there is liberty.' Please excuse me, sir; I will never intrude again."

"O, no intrusion, madam, come again."

"Thank you; I will when I can go nowhere else."

As she passed on, choked with deep emotion, a gentleman stepped to her side, and said, "Don't weep, lady; I know what you have passed through; but they have dealt gently with you. I have

127

known them to tell ladies of great refinement and talent to stop and sit down, when the room has been full of people, but as true as you live, I feel that that is just what the Fulton-street meeting wants, to make it a power greater than it ever has been."[1]

Jarena Lee was a member of the African Methodist Episcopal Church, a denomination begun by Richard Allen as a result of his frustration with the racist practices of the Methodist Church in the late eighteenth century. She felt called to preach, but at first suspected this was the voice of Satan rather than of God. On her way to see Richard Allen she felt so agitated and frightened that she almost turned back, but when she reached his door, she felt at peace.

I now told him, that the Lord had revealed it to me, that I must preach the gospel. He replied, by asking, in what sphere I wished to move in? I said, among the Methodists. [Allen mentioned a woman who had received permission from her pastor to speak at prayer meetings.] But as to women preaching, he said that our Discipline knew nothing at all about it—that it did not call for women preachers. This I was glad to hear, because it removed the fear of the cross—but no sooner did this feeling cross my mind, than I found that a love of souls had in a measure departed from me; that holy energy which burned within me, as a fire, began to be smothered. . . .

O how careful ought we to be, lest through our by-laws of church government and discipline, we bring into disrepute even the word of life. For as unseemly as it may appear now-a-days for a woman to preach, it should be remembered that nothing is impossible with God. And why should it be thought impossible, heterodox, or improper for a woman to preach? seeing the Saviour died for the woman as well as for the man.

If the man may preach, because the Saviour died for him, why not the woman? seeing he died for her also. Is he not a whole Saviour, instead of a half one? as those who hold it wrong for a woman to preach, would seem to make it appear.[2]

These women were deeply committed to the church and to the Christian faith. They were not trying to prove a point. They had no agenda. They were simply responding to God's call to preach. The church said "No." Not, "You do not have the gifts," but rather, "No, we do not allow women to do that." Jarena Lee and Margaret Van Cott found in the church a connection with God, meaningful spiritual growth, and a sense of community; but when they took the next step toward the ministry, the church said, "No. There are limits to what women can do."

Many women have grown up in the church and found it a place of warmth, acceptance, and encouragement. They may have learned leadership skills in the youth group and been intrigued by the biblical stories. At some point in their lives they experienced a call to the ministry. They wanted to study the Bible and theology, they wanted to be present for people at significant times in their lives, and they wanted to give something back to the church that had given so much to them. And the church often said, "No. You cannot use your gifts here. The church does not need you in the pulpit, but you can teach Sunday school and work in the kitchen." Perhaps the most damaging words the church has said to women are these: "You are mistaken. Your call is not genuine. God does not call women."

Many of the women who encourage the church to rethink its stance on women's ordination are not the radical feminists they are often labeled as, but women who care deeply about the church. They feel such a profound sense of call that they do what they must in order to respond to God. The stories of pioneering women pastors do not suggest that they have an axe to grind or a big ego they are trying to satisfy. They would find it easier to do something else, but they do not have a choice.

Women whose call to the ministry is rejected have an obvious reason for dissatisfaction with the church, but the dis-ease is not limited to aspiring clergy. Other women have expressed a similar ambivalence. At times the church is a source of friendship, spiritual nurture, intellectual challenge, and meaningful worship. At other times women feel as if they will suffocate because the language and worship are so exclusively male and because they are not permitted to participate equally in the worship and sacramental life of the church. Rosemary Radford Ruether vividly described the frustration some women feel.

> Women in contemporary churches are suffering from linguistic deprivation and eucharistic famine. They can no longer nurture their souls in alienating words that ignore or systematically deny their existence. They are starved for the words of life, for symbolic forms that fully and wholeheartedly affirm their personhood and speak truth about the evils of sexism and the possibilities of a future beyond patriarchy. They desperately need primary communities that nurture their journey into wholeness, rather than constantly negating and thwarting it.[3]

Three areas of church life have been particularly challenging for women: worship and liturgy, power and authority, and the sacraments.

The basic pattern and content of the worship service can be profoundly unwelcoming to women. If men are in charge of everything; if all the language is about men; and if God is always spoken of as King, Father and He, women may not feel included. While some churches allow women to be elders, ushers, liturgists, and ministers, even these churches often pray to "our Father, who art in heaven" and affirm their belief in "God the Father Almighty." Some people never notice these language patterns. Others find that the maleness makes it difficult to worship.

Some women pose a second set of questions concerning the locus of power and authority in the church. Who makes the decisions? Who sets the agenda? Women rarely lack informal power in the church, and, in fact, the "mothers of the church" are often a force to be reckoned with. In most congregations women have ways to express their opinions and get things done. Increasingly in mainline denominations women serve as members of the session, vestry, or church board; but for centuries women did not have access to this official, recognized power in the church. In most churches, leadership was a men's club up until thirty or forty years ago. An analysis of denominational structures at all levels still demonstrates this kind of male domination. Women may constitute 60 percent of the church membership, but never constitute 60 percent of the delegates to a governing body. Women may be a majority in the pews and possibly in the board room of a congregation, but they are still a minority in the denominational headquarters and in the general assemblies or conventions. Women have their power, certainly; but it is often indirect and confined to certain spheres.

Some women lack even this power. A few congregations do not permit women to vote on church business. Some congregations refuse to elect women to offices of leadership. Women are welcome to teach Sunday school, assemble the newsletter, run the women's group, and prepare food, but not to teach men, make congregational decisions, or handle the finances. Two African women wrote of their church, "The present malaise in the church might be due to the fact that it has refused to allow women to function normally in the church but has reduced them to all-purpose workers, for example, fund-raisers and rally organizers."[4] In 1968 Mary Daly lamented the fact that although women had made great strides in the professions, they were still excluded from the life of the church. She wrote, "Indeed, at this point in history the Church is in the somewhat comical position of applauding women's legal, professional and political emancipation in secular society while keeping them in the basement of its own edifice."[5] By refusing to use all the gifts of women, the church has denied itself many talents and abilities and perhaps contributed to its own weakness.

Closely linked to both worship and power is the role of the sacraments in the life of the church. Feminist theologians point to the church's sacramental system as evidence of its underlying and pervasive sexism. Infants are baptized in the name of the Father, Son, and Holy Spirit. What does it mean to initiate a girl into a church and a faith whose rituals, symbols, and central figures are all male? Will girls ever find a place in this church? Will it welcome them? Baptism is supposed to be a sign of inclusion and incorporation into the body of Christ, but one could ask if women are fully incorporated or if they become not quite full members. Some Roman Catholic women wear pins that say, "Ordain women or stop baptizing them." They wonder what baptism means if baptized women, who have received the forgiving grace of God, are still not fit for ordination.

A similar question has been raised about profession of faith in the Christian Reformed Church. Like the sacrament of confirmation in the Catholic Church, this ceremony marks the time when a teenager professes his or her faith and desire to be a member of the church. When this denomination was debating women's ordination, women pointed out that young women who joined the Christian Reformed Church were supposedly admitted to all the rights and privileges of church membership. The reality for many years was that women were not admitted to the privilege of ordination. Was the church speaking falsely?

The Eucharist, or Communion, is intended to be a shared meal for the community, a sign of being welcomed and included at God's table. Women have always been allowed to receive the bread and the cup, but only in the last 150 years and only in some traditions have they been allowed to celebrate or officiate at the meal. Even distributing elements already consecrated by the clergy was considered a male privilege until recently. In some Protestant churches women are allowed to cut bread into cubes and pour grape juice into cups, but once the elements leave the church kitchen they are apparently too holy for women to touch. The church sends a disturbing message to women when it allows them to make coffee, prepare potluck dinners, set tables and clean up after meals that take place in the church, but does not allow them to celebrate the Lord's Supper. Can the Eucharist be a meal of oneness when some members are more equal than others?

Ordination, despite being open to women in some churches, is still a profoundly male event. In the Roman Catholic Church, a group of male priests pass on their authority to other men. Even in Protestant churches where women have been allowed to enter the ministry, it is likely that men determine the criteria for ordination and decide who can be ordained.

131

At my ordination service there were no clergywomen present for the laying on of hands. The presiding officer failed to change the male pronouns in the liturgy and kept talking about me as a him. "Almighty God, our heavenly Father, who calls men to this holy office, enlighten thy servant with thy Spirit; strengthen him with thy hand; and so govern him in thy ministry that he may decently and fruitfully walk therein."[6] As I knelt there in the midst of all those men, I could also feel the hand of Brian, my friend from seminary, gently squeezing my neck whenever a "he" was spoken, as if to remind me that I was still included.

At the ordination services of some of my women students and friends, several of them have noted how nice it is to see nylons and high heels in the midst of all the suit pants and wing tip shoes. The presence of women at these sacramental events says something significant about who is included. Yet there is always the question, why aren't there more women? Why are the women's shoes unusual? Should women be content with a few tokens when the structures are so overwhelmingly male?

Sacraments seem to give men power that is denied to women. Men have the power to perform the sacraments and to decide who receives them. The imagery and liturgical forms are often male, and the overall impression is of power and grace being doled out from on high. At times the sacraments seem to be less the work of the whole church and more a demonstration of the power of the hierarchy to decide who is in and who is out.

Feminists find the vision of the nature of the church that is inherent in these practices very unfriendly to women. Tradition supports their exclusion and criticizes those who work for change. The church hierarchy excludes women from positions of power and presumes to make decisions for them and to demand obedience. Preservation of the institution at all costs seems to be a core value. Many women find it deeply offensive to hear that holy things and activities need to be protected from unholy women. If the church is unwilling to grant women full equality within the church and at times silences or disciplines those who disagree, is there any hope for women in the church?

The Choice to Leave the Church

Some feminists encourage women to leave the church, arguing that it is hopelessly patriarchal and will never change. In 1968 Mary Daly published *The Church and the Second Sex*, a pointed analysis of the role of women in the Roman Catholic Church. Her work led to a tenure battle at the Roman Catholic college where she taught, although she received a great deal of student support and was eventually granted tenure. Her own experience with the church, therefore, was stormy. In 1971 she became the first woman to preach at a Sunday service at Harvard Memorial Church in its 336-year history. In her sermon she described the deep and persistent sexism of the church, and she challenged the women in attendance to leave the church rather than suffer continued slavery.

> We have to go out from the land of our fathers into an unknown place. We can this morning demonstrate our exodus from sexist religion—a break which for many of us has already taken place spiritually. We can give physical expression to our exodus community, to the fact that we must go away.
>
> We cannot really belong to institutional religion as it exists. It isn't good enough to be token preachers. It isn't good enough to have our energies drained and co-opted. Singing sexist hymns, praying to a male god breaks our spirit, makes us less than human. The crushing weight of this tradition, of this power structure, tells us that *we do not even exist.*
>
> The women's movement is an exodus community. Its basis is not merely in the promise given to our fathers thousands of years ago. Rather its source is in the unfulfilled promise of our mothers' lives, whose history was never recorded. Its source is in the promise of our sisters whose voices have been robbed from them, and in our own promise, our latent creativity. We can affirm now our promise and our exodus as we walk into a future that will be our *own* future.
>
> Sisters—and brothers, if there are any here: Our time has come. We will take our own place in the sun. We will leave behind the centuries of silence and darkness. Let us affirm our faith in ourselves and our will to transcendence by rising and walking out together.[7]

Some women choose to leave the church because they feel completely hopeless about its future. It appears to be so entrenched in its patriarchal ways that it will not be able to change. Even if the priesthood or ministry would someday be open to women, they fear that the underlying assumptions about both the church and women will be so strong that women will never find a comfortable home within the church.

Others choose to leave because the church has already caused them pain and they refuse to take it anymore. For some women the pain comes because the church refuses to acknowledge their call. Other women feel that they have been allowed into the system as tokens, but are not allowed to fully exercise their gifts. Some traditions will allow women to be youth pastors, for example, but do not recognize or affirm their abilities to preach and lead. Some women do not identify one particular cause of pain and anger, but they respond to the failings of the church with a constant sense of irritation and frustration that saps their energy and their passion for the gospel. Some women say they no longer feel hurt by the church because they have developed ways to protect themselves, but they often report a deep sense of exhaustion. They are weary of the sexism and the exclusion, and they no longer have the energy to stay and fight.

Some feminist theologians argue that the church harms women not only by exclusion, but also by its activities and rituals. Mary Daly wrote of liturgy and sacraments, "The rituals of patriarchy *do* create false needs, such as the need to lean on father-figures instead of finding strength in the self, or the need for compulsive 'self-sacrifice' because one is brainwashed into thinking that one is sinful and 'unworthy.' "[8] Daly also argued that even feminist liturgy is a contradiction in terms because the liturgical forms belong to the patriarchal church, because liturgy has long been used to support sexism, and because tinkering with the language will not bring about substantive change. Joanne Carlson Brown and Rebecca Parker observed that those women who stay because they think that someday they will make a difference are deluding themselves:

> The women who stay are as surely victimized and abused as any battered woman. The reasons given by women who stay in the church are the same as those coming from women who remain in battering situations: they don't mean it; they said they were sorry and would be better; they need me/us; we can fix it if we just try harder and are better; I'd leave but how can I survive outside; we have nowhere else to go. . . . Our continuing presence in the church is a sign of the depth of our oppression.[9]

Some feminists believe that in view of the active opposition women often receive from the pope and from other church structures, women must recognize the fact that the church will never change and will never fully appreciate them. The church appears to be the enemy, and there are no good reasons why women should expend so much effort to be accepted by an institution that has been so hurtful and destructive.

Feminist Revisioning of the Church as the People of God

Some readers may protest that their experience of the church has been very different. For them the church has been a welcoming and gracious community, even a home. There may be aspects of the church they would like to change, but they do not want to leave because in the midst of the clericalism, sexism, and hierarchy, they see glimmers of hope. When the church is able to appreciate the tradition without being constrained by it, when the church is more engaged in self-giving than in self-defense, and when the church helps people worship in meaningful ways, it can be a positive place for women.

Feminist theologians have questioned the traditional definition of the church as guardian of the truth and suggested that the church need not be quite so zealous for God's honor and the purity of the gospel. The role of the church is not to determine who is in and out, right and wrong, but to be present in the world to love, serve, and help the good news be heard and seen and experienced. God can care for and preserve God's church. If the church expended less effort debating the fine points of theology and polity, it might have more creative energy to be God's hands and feet in the world, a task that has often been neglected.

The feminist vision of the church places far less emphasis on the church's authority because the essence of the church is not a uniform belief system or a set of rules that must be obeyed. The church does not need a man at the top to make all its decisions. The church has taken far too much power upon itself and has claimed to have far more authority to transmit the grace of God than perhaps God ever intended. Although the church often does function as a channel for God's voice, power, and mercy, the church is not the only way to meet God. God's grace can be received without the mediation of a priest. God's will can be discerned without the instruction of a pastor. Tradition may be informative, but it is not always right and it does not have the last word. God pours out wisdom and compassion in many and varied ways. The church and the clergy cannot control or direct the flow of grace because it is God's grace, not theirs.

The church has more room for diversity than the institution and its leaders have often permitted. The history of the church is sometimes presented in a way that suggests that there is one right answer. Some people assume, for example, that after 325, when the Council of Nicaea decided that Jesus was of the same substance as God, everyone agreed and never challenged the decision again. There was then and has been ever since a great deal of disagreement and debate over theological issues. Feminist theologians argue that people do not have to agree about everything in order to be faithful Christians and church members. Some diversity of opinion is possible as long as people share the same basic commitment to the gospel. Preserving boundaries and purity is not as important as living together in the midst of diversity.

135

Feminist theologian Letty Russell used the image of the church in the round to describe the ideal church community. Perhaps the most common church structure is a large building where all the pews face forward and all attention is focused on the minister at the front who preaches from an elevated pulpit. He looks down at the people, who must look up at him. The people cannot see each others' faces, only the backs of heads. Feminist theologians believe that worship would be different if worshipers sat in a circle where they could see each other and if the minister stood at their level, as one of them. A church in the round allows greater participation by the people in worship, thus it is less of a clerical performance and more of a communal experience. A church in the round enables the whole church to participate in making decisions and setting goals rather than simply carrying out the mandates of the clergy. A church in the round values all its members and does not discriminate based on wealth, appearance, intellectual abilities, or social skills. There is a place for everyone. Ideally, people see, meet, and know each other; consequently the church can be a supportive community, not simply a social club or a place where one performs one's duty to God and then is free for the remainder of the week.

When contemporary churches evaluate their effectiveness, they often use numbers—membership, giving, attendance, or the size of the latest building project. A "successful" church has numbers that increase each year. Feminist theologians suggest criteria that are less quantifiable or at least less often deemed worthy of measurement. How many hours do church members spend tutoring children, lobbying for welfare reform, or working in a soup kitchen? Russell wrote, "The measure of the adequacy of the life of a church is how it is connected to those on the margin, whether those the NRSV calls 'the least of these who are members of my family' are receiving the attention to their needs for justice and hope (Matt 25:40)"[10] In a world full of conflict, racism, exclusion, homophobia, and other signs of brokenness, is the church a place of safety and genuine care? Is the church hospitable to those who are different or difficult? Does the church not only offer charity to the poor, but actively seek justice for them? Is the church concerned primarily with its own growth and the care of its own members, or is it trying to bring a measure of healing and wholeness to a broken world?

Why Stay?

A church that practices justice and hospitality, invites questions, welcomes all God's people, and encourages community rather than hierarchy would be easy for feminists to attend. Some women have found such a church. However, a surprising number of feminists choose to stay in churches they find at best ambiguous and at worst difficult. They remain active and committed members of the Roman Catholic Church, of conservative Protestant churches, and of mainline churches that assume they are more progressive than they really are. Their choice sparks a number of difficult questions. Why stay in a church that is so far from ideal? Why stay in a church that denies women the right of ordination? Why stay in a church where women experience "linguistic deprivation and eucharistic famine?" And if women do stay in the church, is it possible to work through the anger and frustration and live creatively and joyfully?

One simple, but powerful, response to "Why stay?" is, "Because it is my church." Women who have been reared in or who have chosen a particular tradition or congregation feel a sense of history in and connection with it. They appreciate its liturgy and feel a sense of community with God's people. They have found in the church a place of growth and healing, they believe the church can change, and they are unwilling to give up a place that is meaningful to them.

A second reason to stay is because it is God's church. Women have been able to tolerate sexism, exclusive language, and second class citizenship because they encounter God in church. Feminist theologians recognize that God's body the church is a human institution and as such is sinful and limited. The deformities of the church are not God's will, but the result of human imperfection. The church must be called back to God's original intentions for it. Feminists will not concede the power of defining the church to those who advocate the most conservative position, but continue to challenge the church to live out a different vision.

Christian feminists also stay in the church because they believe that the essential message of the gospel proclaims freedom and justice. Early in her career, before she became disillusioned with the church, Mary Daly wrote, "The equal dignity and rights of all human beings as persons is of the essence of the Christian message."[11] Elisabeth Schüssler Fiorenza described her roots in the church:

> My own experience as a woman who grew up in the Catholic tradition compels me to question the assertion that maleness is the essence of the Christian faith and theology. In spite of the masculine terminology of prayers, catechism, and liturgy, and in spite of blatant patriarchal male spiritual guidance, my commitment to Christian faith and love first led me to question the feminine cultural role that parents, school, and church had taught me to accept and to internalize. My vision of Christian life, responsibility, and

community compelled me to reject the culturally imposed role of women and not vice versa. What was this liberating vision that came to me despite all patriarchal pious packaging and sexist theological systematization?[12]

This liberating vision keeps many feminists in the church. They believe that the church at its core challenges the status quo and affirms equality and justice for all God's people. This means that the church should actively lead in the struggle for human rights, not simply follow when it is safe to do so. The church should not passively accept the status quo, whether beliefs about slavery or race or women or homosexuality, but lead society to a different vision. The church should be an agent of change. It should not be content to live out the tradition in the old ways. Many feminists feel a strong sense of vocation to remain in the church and encourage it to be transformed.

In But Still Out

Transformation almost always requires a critique of the status quo, which is why feminist theologians are so often accused of being overly critical. Elisabeth Schüssler Fiorenza recalled an encounter with a bishop who affirmed her insights about the condition of the church, but asked that she not name its wounds so pointedly. He preferred to cover up those wounds and preserve the appearance of a healthy, unified church. She replied that healing would be possible only after wounds were cleansed and evil was cut out.[13] Feminist theologians insist that commitment to the church does not mean absolute loyalty, full agreement, and the absence of criticism. Choosing to stay usually involves a commitment to work for the transformation of the church. Feminist theologians take the church to task on many points, but most of them care deeply about the church and want it to be all that it can be as the people of God. It is not easy to both stay in the church and insist that it needs to be changed, and many women pay an enormous price for their efforts. Feminist theologians are a prophetic voice within the church calling for change; but it is no easy or comfortable task to be a prophet, and the church rarely appreciates the prophetic voices within.

Feminist theologians have asked the church to begin the process of transformation with repentance. Schüssler Fiorenza asked that the Roman Catholic Church "publicly and officially confess that it has wronged women."[14] The church must repent of its poor treatment of women "because the credibility of the Christian gospel and church is at stake."[15] Quick answers and easy reconciliation will not heal centuries of alienation. There is no peace without justice and no reconciliation without honest repentance.

Feminist theologians have also noticed the difficulty of participating in an institution that has been happy to receive labor and money from women, but has allowed them little in return. Women were welcomed in the church as long as they were cooperative, hard-working, obedient, and nice; but they were not supposed to challenge the decisions of the institution. Sometimes women circumvented the structures of the church, as in the nineteenth century when Protestant missionary societies refused to send unmarried women to the mission fields to evangelize women. Women formed their own missionary societies and raised money by saving leftover coins from household expenses. They were remarkably successful, and by the 1920s and 1930s many of these societies had been integrated into denominational boards, which took the women's money but gave them only limited leadership and authority. In the Roman Catholic Church cloistered nuns who spent their lives in prayer were acceptable; but when they wanted to teach or staff hospitals, the hierarchy often resisted their attempt to be of more service to the world and encouraged the nuns to remain safe in the cloister. Many orders developed creative ways to live out their vocation despite the lack of support.

Women have developed a number of strategies for dealing with the ambiguity they experience with the church. Some women express their disagreement with the church while officially retaining membership, which Miriam Therese Winter labeled "defecting in place."[16] She and her colleagues reported that many of the women they surveyed did not attend their church regularly and instead formed groups of women for worship, study, and prayer. They often donated money to women-friendly organizations rather than to the church.

Some women choose more dramatic ways to demonstrate their resistance to the traditional structures of the church. Elizabeth Schüssler Fiorenza suggested that women refuse to participate in a Eucharist as a kind of spiritual hunger strike. Some Roman Catholic women have celebrated Eucharist without a priest, arguing that the clergy does not own the sacrament. Some women are ordained before their denominations officially approve the practice. Other women simply leave one denomination for another that allows them to use their gifts.

Some women have chosen to deal with the ambiguity of the church by creating alternative worshiping communities, sometimes called Women-Church. These women feel starved in the church, but are deeply committed to Christianity. They want to worship in a community, but find the institutional church oppressive and destructive. They cannot wait for the church to reform itself enough to provide spiritual sustenance for them. They choose to find a separate place where they can experience a supportive community and engage in meaningful theological reflection and creative worship. They want to be in a space that provides an alternative to the hierarchy and clericalism of the traditional church and that does not offend them with exclusive language or practice.

As part of their worship experience, WomenChurch groups have developed creative rituals celebrating or mourning specific life experiences of women, such as menopause, old age, pregnancy, stillbirth, or rape. Although critics have charged that such rituals encourage women to worship themselves, their bodies, or the goddess, rather than God, participants report that these worship experiences can be a powerful way to encounter God, to find grace and healing, and to build strong relationships with other women. WomenChurch groups have helped women learn to trust and value each other and to meet God in new ways. They continue to hope that the church will change, but they believe that their spiritual well-being requires a safer and more nurturing space than they have found in the traditional church. Women in these groups do not necessarily see men as the enemy, but they recognize the depth of patriarchy and believe that separate space often provides the energy to continue the fight against oppression.[17]

One of the dangers of this dual role of being both a member and a critic of the church is the deep sense of exhaustion that often comes from a constant struggle. Those who speak with a prophetic voice find that they live with a lot of anger and are always physically and emotionally prepared for a fight. But they stay because sometimes the church gets it right and women experience a deep sense of joy and belonging. On the evening of my graduation from seminary, my husband and I drove to the church I had been serving for the past two years. I thought we were meeting friends to go to a baseball game. To my great surprise and delight, the congregation was gathered for a surprise party to celebrate my graduation and my time in their midst. The affirmation and love were overwhelming to me, and I still consider this congregation one of the great gifts in my life. At its best, the church can be a loving, life-giving place for the people of God.

Ministry and Ordination

The issue of women's role in the church, specifically whether they can be ordained and serve in leadership positions, has sparked much discussion among feminists. Many of the arguments for and against women's ordination have been discussed in other chapters of the book, so they will be only briefly summarized here.

Many Protestants argue that the Bible prohibits women from holding leadership positions in the church. They appeal to the hierarchy in Genesis and to New Testament passages such as 1 Corinthians 14:34-5; 1 Timothy 2:11-15; and Ephesians 5:22-24. They believe that the Bible says clearly that women are not permitted to speak in church or to have authority over men.

Many Roman Catholic and Orthodox Christians argue that tradition does not permit women to be priests. Jesus never ordained women, and therefore the church should not ordain women. Jesus was a man and priests must represent and resemble him. The intellectual and spiritual deficits inherent in female nature renders women unfit for ministry. Thomas Aquinas argued that women are in a state of subjection and cannot receive the sacrament of ordination. The sacrament would be invalid for them because the authority granted to priests simply cannot be given to a woman. He acknowledged that women could be prophets, as they were in Scripture, but he considered prophecy a gift from God rather than a sacrament. The fact that women served as abbesses did not justify ordination because abbesses simply possessed delegated authority over other women so that monks would not have close contact with nuns. He acknowledged that Deborah possessed authority in her role as judge, but it was in secular matters rather than in priestly ones. God grants occasional temporal authority to a woman, but does not want them to have spiritual authority.[18]

Opponents of women's ordination also cite a number of ecclesiastical arguments in defense of their position. The church is not ready for women in leadership. The tender conscience of those who oppose women's ordination cannot be violated. If women are allowed to be ordained, some people will leave the church and congregations or denominations may divide. The church is already composed of a majority of women, and if women are allowed to be ordained, they will gain more power in the church and more men will leave. Feminization of the church will result in further loss of power and prestige for male priests and clergy. Ministry will become a pink-collar profession and will no longer be respected.

Other arguments are less theological, but equally influential. One of the most common is "We have never done it that way before." Some of the opposition to women's leadership is rooted in stereotypical assumptions about the nature and abilities of men and women. Men are designed to lead and organize. Women are designed to follow and nurture. Men are spiritual and intellectual beings. Women are bodily and emotional beings. It seems unnatural for women to exercise authority. It does not feel right to have a woman in charge, telling men what to do.

Women's sexuality makes their handling of the holy things offensive in a way that is not true for men. One troubled critic asked, "Can you imagine a pregnant woman at the altar?" and the obvious answer was no. Samuel Johnson summarized many of these attitudes when he observed: "A woman's preaching is like a dog walking on his hinder legs. It is not done well; but you are surprised to find it done at all."[19] Critics charge that ordination for women is unnatural and inappropriate, and that women enter the ministry because of selfishness and egoism rather than because of a genuine call.

Most feminist theologians respond to these objections by affirming the equality of women and men, the giftedness of women for ministry, and God's call to women. They challenge the church to fully welcome women into all offices of the church because it is the just thing to do, not because there is a shortage of male priests, as in the Roman Catholic Church, or because the ordained ministry has lost much its former prestige, as in many Protestant churches.

Feminist theologians also recognize that the ordination of women carries with it some problems, particularly the idea that ordination admits clergy into a special caste, with privileges and duties that are denied to other Christians. In varying degrees depending on the denomination, clergy are considered closer to God, more spiritual, and better able to pray, preach, interpret Scripture, and run the church. Clericalism perpetuates patriarchy by giving clergy power over dependent and subordinate laypeople, much as fathers have power over their children. Ordination contributes to the disempowerment of the laity when it endows clergy with authority to communicate the word of God and pass on the traditions of the church, while telling laypeople that faith is simple and that they should believe what they are told and accept the decisions of the clergy. An overemphasis on clerical power discourages laypeople from thinking for themselves, asking difficult questions, and disagreeing with clerical decisions.[20]

Some feminist theologians fear that simply letting women into the ranks of the clergy will not significantly transform the church. Only a complete restructuring will create a more inclusive and participatory church, and permitting a few women into the church's power structures is unlikely to bring about the change that is necessary. Admitting a few women might give the false impression that the church has already changed, thus delaying transformation rather than promoting it.

Women as Clergy

Despite these concerns about ordination and clericalism, women are attending seminary and entering the ministry in substantial numbers.

Their presence raises some interesting questions. Do women do ministry differently? Are they more nurturing? Less authoritarian? Do they use power differently? Do they bring any distinctive gifts?

A student visited a church where a woman served as the associate pastor and observed that the woman's feminine nature made her more nurturing and caring than the male senior pastor was. In this case it may have been true, but did these abilities come from her female nature? If so, does that mean that all women are more nurturing and caring than men? Such a conclusion could suggest that women should always serve as associate pastors in charge of congregational care and education, since that is the area of their giftedness, while men should always be senior pastors, since they excel at leadership and administration. Overemphasizing so-called feminine traits in such a way may be detrimental to women in the long run.

Women have diverse gifts just as men do. Some are excellent preachers; some are average. Some are very intuitive and easily able to care for people; some find that more difficult. Some are good administrators; some are not. Pastoral abilities are not gender specific or connected in any way to hormones or reproductive organs. It may be true to say that women are more comfortable as nurturers because they have been taught to be and have been affirmed when they did it well. Similarly, men may find it easier to make decisions and run meetings because that is what men are supposed to do. Women may think differently about authority, leadership, and power because these traits have not always been recognized in women. They may emphasize shared power and consensus building because they know how it feels to be denied the opportunity to make decisions and exercise authority. There are female clergy who tend to be authoritative and hierarchical and male clergy who work to empower others. Leadership style has far more to do with personality and socialization than with an X or a Y chromosome.

If men and women are basically the same, why is it so important to have women clergy on a church staff, or women serving on denominational staff, or women leading worship? A complementarity model suggests that men and women have very different gifts based on gender and that neither is complete without the other. His aggression is balanced by her gentleness, and her weakness by his strength. A mutuality model suggests that a female/male leadership team represents, not two halves that need to complete each other, but two whole people, each with gifts and limitations, which symbolizes what diversity means for the church. A worship service led by several men sends a message that men are in charge here. A male and female pastoral team sends a message that the church recognizes the gifts of both men and women.

However, if the man is always the senior pastor who does most of the preaching, it sends a message that women are acceptable in supportive, nurturing, secondary roles, but not as leaders and preachers.

Anna Garlin Spencer, a pastor and educator, wrote in 1912, "A successful woman preacher was once asked, 'what special obstacles have you met as a woman in the ministry?' 'Not one,' she answered, 'except the lack of a minister's wife.' "[21] Most contemporary women clergy have encountered more obstacles than this. Sexism and patriarchy run deep in both church and culture, and much of the resistance to women in leadership is rooted less in the Bible or in tradition than in our sense of what it means to be male and female. Many women clergy have found that people's minds are changed less by debate and rational argument than by encountering women as they preach, teach, care, and administer.

The congregation that I attend recently called a woman to be minister of worship and witness. The local newspaper wrote a story about her, and a television station taped her installation service and reported it on the evening news. Such stories always emphasize the great strides women are making and the growing acceptance they find in churches. Many women clergy long for the day when women become senior pastors or denominational executives without any video cameras or fanfare, when gender is no longer such an issue, and when we can no longer quickly count the number of women in leadership. Perhaps then, when the church is truly using the gifts of all its members, God's holy energy will no longer be smothered, as it was in Jarena Lee. Perhaps when the church is using the gifts of all its members, it will be a power greater than it ever has been. Perhaps when the church is using the gifts of all its members, a female minister will no longer make the news.

Notes

Introduction

1. Sarah Grimke, "Letters on the Equality of the Sexes and the Condition of Women," in *Feminism: The Essential Historical Writings*, ed. Miriam Schneir (New York: Vintage Books, 1972), 37-38.

2. Jesus did not ordain men to church office either. The notion of ordination and church office arose several decades later.

1. An Introduction to Feminist Theology

1. Julian of Norwich, *Showings* (New York: Paulist Press, 1978), 296.

2. Carter Heyward, *Our Passion for Justice* (New York: Pilgrim Press, 1984), 6.

3. Regina Coll, *Christianity and Feminism in Conversation* (Mystic, Conn.: Twenty-Third Publications, 1994), 17.

4. Mary Daly, *Beyond God the Father: Toward a Philosophy of Women's Liberation* (Boston: Beacon Press, 1973), 4.

5. The same is true for cultural examples of sexism. As a child I loved the television version of *Cinderella*, but when my daughter watched the video recently I found the sexism disturbing. The prince sings, "Do I love you because you're beautiful, or are you beautiful because I love you?" It was impossible for me to revisit my previous delight in the movie.

6. Rosemary Radford Ruether, "The Future of Feminist Theology in the Academy," *Journal of the American Academy of Religion* 53:3, (1985), 703-13.

7. Roberta Bondi, *Memories of God: Theological Reflections on a Life* (Nashville: Abingdon Press, 1995), 11.

8. Chung Hyun Kyung, *Struggle to Be the Sun Again: Introducing Asian Women's Theology* (Maryknoll: Orbis Books, 1990), 87.

9. Daphne Hampson, *Theology and Feminism* (Cambridge, Mass.: Basil Blackwell, 1990), 9; Daly, *Beyond God the Father*, 74.

10. Anne E. Carr, *Transforming Grace: Christian Tradition and Women's Experience* (San Francisco: Harper & Row, 1988), 55.

11. Ivone Gebara, "Women Doing Theology in Latin America," in *Feminist Theology from the Third World: A Reader*, ed. Ursula King (Maryknoll: Orbis Books, 1994), 56-57.

12. Rosemary R. Ruether, *Sexism and God-Talk* (Boston: Beacon Press, 1983), 18-19.

13. Aurelia T. Fule, "Reformed—And Always Reforming?" in *Women and Church*, ed. Melanie May (Grand Rapids: Eerdmans, 1991), 21.

14. Sandra Schneiders, "Feminist Spirituality: Christian Alternative or Alternative to Christianity?" in *Women's Spirituality: Resources for Christian Development*, 2nd ed., ed. Joann W. Conn (New York: Paulist Press, 1996), 53.

15. Virginia Woolf, *A Room of One's Own* (San Diego: Harcourt, Brace, Jovanovich, 1929), 26.

16. Gerda Lerner, *The Creation of Feminist Consciousness: From the Middle Ages to 1870* (New York: Oxford University Press, 1993), 166.

17. Carr, *Transforming Grace*, 93.

18. Gebara, "Women Doing Theology," 51, 56.

19. Delores Williams, *Sisters in the Wilderness: The Challenge of Womanist God-Talk* (Maryknoll: Orbis Books, 1995).

20. Edith Deen, *All of the Women of the Bible* (New York: Harper & Row, 1955), 8-16.

21. Ada M. Isasi-Diaz, *Mujerista Theology: A Theology for the Twenty-First Century* (Maryknoll: Orbis Books, 1996), 60.

22. Rosemary R. Ruether, *To Change the World: Christology and Cultural Criticism* (New York: Crossroad, 1981); Mud Flower Collective, *God's Fierce Whimsy: Christian Feminism and Theological Education*, ed. Carter Heyward (New York: Pilgrim Press, 1985); Susan Thistlethwaite, *Sex, Race, and God: Christian Feminism in Black and Christian Feminism in Black and White* (New York: Crossroad, 1989).

23. Elizabeth A. Johnson, *She Who Is: The Mystery of God in Feminist Theological Discourse* (New York: Crossroad, 1992), 18, 11.

24. Naomi Wolf, *Fire with Fire* (Toronto: Random House of Canada, 1993); Gebara, "Women Doing Theology," 54.

25. Virginia Fabella and Mercy A. Oduyoye, "Introduction," *With Passion and Compassion*, x.

2. Feminist Perspectives on the Bible

1. Mexico Conference, "Final Document on Doing Theology from Third World Women's Perspective," in *Feminist Theology from the Third World: A Reader*, ed. Ursula King (Maryknoll: Orbis Books, 1994), 38-39.

2. Rigoberta Menchu, "The Bible and Self-Defense: The Examples of Judith, Moses, and David," in *Feminist Theology From the Third World*, 186-87.

3. Chung Hyun Kyung, *Struggle to Be the Sun Again: Introducing Asian Women's Theology* (Maryknoll: Orbis Books, 1990), 45.

4. Cheryl J. Sanders, "Black Women in Biblical Perspective: Resistance, Affirmation, and Empowerment," in *Living the Intersection: Womanism and Afrocentrism in Theology*, ed. Cheryl J. Sanders (Minneapolis: Augsburg Fortress, 1995), 126.

5. Renita J. Weems, "Reading *Her Way* Through the Struggle: African American Women and the Bible," in *Stony the Road We Trod: African American Biblical Interpretation*, ed. Cain H. Felder (Minneapolis: Augsburg Fortress, 1991), 77.

6. Phyllis Trible, "Depatriarchalizing in the Biblical Tradition," *Journal of the American Academy of Religion*, XLI (March 1973), 30-48; Mary Daly, *Beyond God the Father: Toward a Philosophy of Women's Liberation* (Boston: Beacon Press, 1973), 206.

7. Sandra Schneiders, *Beyond Patching: Faith and Feminism in the Catholic Church* (New York: Paulist Press, 1991), 52.

8. Johanna W. Van-Wijk Bos, *Reimagining God: The Case for Scriptural Diversity* (Louisville: Westminster/John Knox Press, 1995), 10.

9. Johanna W. Van-Wijk Bos, *Reformed and Feminist: A Challenge to the Church* (Louisville: Westminster/John Knox Press, 1991), 65.

10. Letty M. Russell, ed., *Feminist Interpretation of the Bible* (Philadelphia: Westminster/John Knox Press, 1985), 141.

11. Van-Wijk Bos, *Reformed and Feminist*, 37.

12. Authority can be defined as legitimated power. The chairperson of my department has legitimate power to tell me what to teach and to evaluate my work. A close friend can give me legitimate advice, but has no power to make me follow it. A mugger has the power to make me give up my wallet, but this power is not legitimate or valid. See Paul Fries, "Inspiration and Authority: The Reformed Church Engages Modernity," in *Word and World: Reformed Theology in America*, ed. James Van Hoeven (Grand Rapids: Eerdmans, 1986), 86.

13. Claudia Camp, "Feminist Theological Hermeneutics: Canon and Christian Identity," in *Searching the Scriptures*, vol. 1, *A Feminist Introduction*, ed. Elisabeth S. Fiorenza (New York: Crossroad, 1993), 1:162.

14. Weems, pp. 70-71.

15. Ada M. Isasi-Diaz, *"La Palabra de Dios en Nosotras*—The Word of God in Us," *Searching the Scriptures*, 1:89.

16. Russell, "Reading *Her Way* Through the Struggle," 138.

17. Gerda Lerner, *The Creation of Feminist Consciousness: From the Middle Ages to 1870* (New York: Oxford University Press, 1993), 138.

18. For a helpful explanation of Leviticus and other biblical texts about sexual ethics, see L. William Countryman, *Dirt, Greed, and Sex: Sexual Ethics in the New Testament and Their Implications for Today* (Philadelphia: Fortress Press, 1988).

19. Elisabeth S. Fiorenza, *In Memory of Her: A Feminist Theological Reconstruction of Christian Origins* (New York: Crossroad, 1985), 284-334.

20. Rita N. Brock, "Dusting the Bible on the Floor: A Hermeneutics of Wisdom," *Searching the Scriptures*, 1:72.

21. Teresa Okure, "Women in the Bible," in *With Passion and Compassion: Third World Women Doing Theology*, ed. Virginia Fabella and Mercy Amba Oduyoye (Maryknoll: Orbis Books, 1988), 52.

22. Elsa Tamez, "Women's Rereading of the Bible," in *Feminist Theology from the Third World*, 194-95.

23. Rosemary R. Ruether, *Sexism and God-Talk* (Boston: Beacon Press, 1983) 22-33.

24. Schneiders, 54.

25. Tamez, 193.

26. Letty M. Russell, *Household of Freedom* (Philadelphia: Westminster Press, 1987) 49.

27. Okura, 55.

28. Weems, 70-71.

29. Fiorenza, *In Memory of Her.*

30. Isazi-Diaz, 1:87.

31. Weems, 63.

32. Margaret A. Farley, "Feminist Consciousness and the Interpretation of Scripture," in *Feminist Interpretation of the Bible*, 43-44.

33. Kathleen Norris, *Amazing Grace: A Vocabulary of Faith*, ed. Cindy Spiegel (New York: Riverhead Books, 1998), pp. 132-33.

3. Language About God

1. Cited in Paul Smith, *Is It Okay to Call God Mother? Considering the Feminine Face of God* (Peabody, Mass.: Hendrickson Publishers, 1993), 151.

2. Mary Daly, *Beyond God the Father: Toward a Philosophy of Women's Liberation* (Boston: Beacon Press, 1973), 19.

3. Statistics show that fewer people are abused by their mothers, but it does occur. Exclusive use of maternal language for God is therefore equally problematic.

4. Andrew J. Dell'Olio discussed many of the arguments against feminine God language in "Why Not God the Mother?" *Faith and Philosophy,* vol. 15, no. 2, April 1998.

5. Daphne Hampson, *Theology and Feminism* (Cambridge, Mass.: Basil Blackwell, 1990), 151.

6. Elizabeth Achtemeier, "The Impossible Possibility: Evaluating the Feminist Approach to Bible and Theology," *Interpretation,* January 1988, 56.

7. A lectionary is a set of readings from the Old Testament, Psalms, epistles, and Gospels for each Sunday of the church year. Many churches use these readings in worship, and the *Inclusive Language Lectionary* proposed an alternative translation for these without rewriting the entire Bible.

8. Elizabeth A. Johnson uses a similar outline in chapter 6 of *She Who Is: The Mystery of God in Feminist Theological Discourse* (New York: Crossroad, 1994).

9. Columba, "O God, Thou Art the Father," trans. Duncan Macgregor, *The Hymnbook,* p. 89.

10. Cited in Johnson, *She Who Is,* 7, 45.

11. Carter Heyward, *Our Passion for Justice* (New York: Pilgrim Press, 1984), 27.

12. Johnson, *She Who Is,* 110; Johanna W. Van-Wijk Bos, *Reimagining God: The Case for Scriptural Diversity* (Louisville: Westminster/John Knox Press, 1991), 95; Elisabeth S. Fiorenza, *Discipleship of Equals: A Critical Feminist Ekklesia-logy of Liberation* (New York: Crossroad, 1993), 210.

13. Van-Wijk Bos, *Reimagining God,* 48.

14. Phyllis Trible, *God and the Rhetoric of Sexuality* (Philadelphia: Fortress Press, 1978), 16.

15. Johanna W. Van-Wijk Bos, "When You Pray Say 'Our Father,' " *Presbyterian Survey,* May 1981, 12; Sallie McFague, *Metaphorical Theology: Models of God in Religious Language* (Philadelphia: Fortress Press, 1982), 9.

16. Cited in Smith, *Is It Okay to Call God Mother?* 63, 61.

17. Johnson, *She Who Is,* 71.

18. Virginia R. Mollenkott, *The Divine Feminine: The Biblical Imagery of God as Female* (New York: Crossroad, 1985), 83-91.

19. Johnson, *She Who Is,* 258.

20. Carol P. Christ, *Rebirth of the Goddess* (Addison-Wesley Publishing Company, 1997), 2.

21. Brian Wren, *What Language Shall I Borrow? God-Talk in Worship: A Male Response to Feminist Theology* (New York: Crossroad, 1991), 146.

22. Sallie McFague, *Models of God: Theology for an Ecological Nuclear Age* (Philadelphia: Fortress, 1987), 157-80.

23. Daly, *Beyond God the Father*, 33-34; Gail Ramshaw, *God Beyond Gender: Feminist Christian God-Language* (Minneapolis: Augsburg Fortress, 1995), 120-26.

24. For examples of the positive effects of feminine God language in women's lives, see Patricia L. Reilly, *A God Who Looks Like Me: Discovering a Woman-Affirming Spirituality* (New York: Ballantine Books, 1995).

25. Anne E. Carr, *Transforming Grace: Christian Tradition and Women's Experience* (San Francisco: Harper and Row, 1988), 134.

26. Van-Wijk Bos, *Reimagining God*, 22.

27. Wren, *What Language Shall I Borrow?* 138.

28. Alice Walker, "God Is Inside You and Inside Everybody Else," in *Weaving the Visions: New Patterns in Feminist Spirituality*, ed. Judith Plaskow and Carol P. Christ (San Francisco: Harper & Row, 1989), 104.

4. Human Nature and Sin

1. Julia O'Faolain and Laura Martines (eds.), *Not in God's Image: Women in History from the Greeks to the Victorians* (Harper and Row, 1973) 130.

2. Ibid., 131-32.

3. Elizabeth Clark and Herbert Richardson (eds.), *Women and Religion: The Original Sourcebook of Women in Christian Thought* (Harper SanFrancisco, 1996) 126-29.

4. O'Faolain and Martines, 167.

5. Ibid., 132.

6. Ibid., 129.

7. Even a theologian such as Aquinas believed that prostitutes provided a necessary outlet for male sexuality. He referred to prostitutes as sewers, essential, but disgusting.

8. A few exceptional women religious in the medieval period functioned as scholars, teachers, and administrators and many others as nuns in cloisters. A few women became queen or held other unusual positions of power.

9. Men also function as both villains and heroes in Disney's movies. When the villain is a male, often the woman is beautiful and sweet, sometimes quite bright and resourceful, such as Belle in *Beauty and the Beast*. More often the women are relatively passive, like the lionesses in *The Lion King*. In general, men have a wider variety of roles, and more depth to their characters. The characters of Pocahontas and Mulan, however, suggest that the images of women are beginning to broaden a bit.

10. Phyllis Trible, "Eve and Adam: Genesis 2–3," in *Womanspirit Rising,* ed. Carol Christ and Judith Plaskow, (San Francisco: Harper and Row, 1979) 74-83.

11. The stories of these women and many others can be found in Ruth Tucker and Walter Liefeld, *Daughters of the Church* (Grand Rapids: Academic Books, 1987).

12. See the discussion of Margaret Mead's work in Valerie Saiving, "The Human Situation: A Feminine View," in *Womanspirit Rising: A Feminist Reader in Religion,* ed. Carol P. Christ and Judith Plaskow (San Francisco: Harper & Row, 1979), 28-29, 34-35.

13. Saiving, "The Human Situation," 30-32.

14. Mary S. Van Leeuwen, *Gender and Grace* (Downers Grove: Inter-Varsity Press, 1990), 75-105.

15. Daphne Hampson, *Theology and Feminism* (Cambridge, Mass.: Basil Blackwell, 1990), 31.

16. Martin Luther, "Lectures on Genesis," *Luther's Works,* vol. 1, ed. Jaroslav Pelikan (St. Louis: Concordia Publishing House, 1958), reprinted in *Women and Religion: The Original Source book of Women in Christian Thought,* ed. Elizabeth A. Clark and Herbert W., Richardson (San Francisco: HarperSanFrancisco, 1996), 167-68.

17. Trible, *God and the Rhetoric of Sexuality* (Philadelphia: Fortress Press, 1978), 79.

18. Ibid., 80.

19. Mary A. O'Neill, "The Mystery of Being Human Together," in *Freeing Theology: The Essentials of Theology in Feminist Perspective,* ed. Catherine M. LaCugna (New York: HarperSanFrancisco, 1993), 142.

20. Bill Leonard, "Forgiving Eve," *The Christian Century* (Nov. 7, 1984), 1040.

21. Sojourner Truth, "Ain't I a Woman?" in *Feminism: The Essential Historical Writings,* ed. Miriam Schneir (New York: Vintage Books, 1972), 95.

22. Saiving, "The Human Situation," 37.

23. Judith Plaskow, *Sex, Sin and Grace: Women's Experience and the Theologies of Reinhold Niebuhr and Paul Tillich* (Washington, D.C.: University Press of America, 1980), 92; Jacquelyn Grant, "The Sin of Servanthood and the Deliverance of Discipleship," in *A Troubling in My Soul: Womanist Perspectives on Evil and Suffering,* ed. Emilie Townes (Maryknoll: Orbis Books, 1993), 215.

24. Therese Souga, "The Christ-Event from the Viewpoint of African Women: A Catholic Perspective," in *With Passion and Compassion: Third World Women Doing Theology,* ed. Virginia Fabella and Mercy A. Oduyoye (Maryknoll: Orbis Books, 1988), 29.

25. Rosemary R. Ruether, *Sexism and God-Talk: Toward a Feminist Theology* (Boston: Beacon Press, 1983), 188-89.

26. Aruna Gnanadason, "Women's Oppression: A Sinful Situation," in *With Passion and Compassion*, 73.

27. Regina Coll, *Christianity and Feminism in Conversation* (Mystic: Conn.: Twenty-Third Publications, 1994), 111.

28. Letty M. Russell, *Human Liberation in a Feminist Perspective: A Theology* (Philadelphia: Westminster Press, 1974), 112.

29. Anne E. Patrick, "Authority, Women, and Church: Reconsidering the Relationship," in *Empowering Authority: The Charisms of Episcopacy and Primacy in the Church Today*, ed. Patrick J. Howell and Gary L. Chamberlain (Kansas City: Sheed & Ward, 1990), 21.

30. Chung Hyun Kyung, *Struggle to Be the Sun Again: Introducing Asian Women's Theology* (Maryknoll: Orbis Books, 1990), 42.

31. Rita N. Brock, *Journeys By Heart: A Christology of Erotic Power* (New York: Crossroad, 1988), 7.

32. Sally Purvis, *The Power of the Cross: Foundations for a Christian Feminist Ethic of Community* (Nashville: Abingdon Press, 1993), 93.

5. Christology

1. Jaroslav Pelikan, *Jesus Through the Centuries: His Place in the History of Culture* (New York: Harper & Row, 1985), 2.

2. Jacquelyn Grant, *White Women's Christ and Black Women's Jesus: Feminist Christology and Womanist Response* (Atlanta: Scholars Press, 1989), 185.

3. Carter Heyward, *Our Passion for Justice* (New York: Pilgrim Press, 1984), 214.

4. Eleanor McLaughlin, "Feminist Christologies: Re-Dressing the Tradition," in *Reconstructing the Christ Symbol: Essays in Feminist Christology*, ed. Maryanne Stevens (New York: Paulist Press, 1994), 127.

5. Leonard Swidler, "Jesus Was a Feminist," *Catholic World*, January 1971, 177-83.

6. Dorothy Sayers, *Are Women Human?* (Grand Rapids: Eerdmans, 1971), 47.

7. Grant, *White Women's Christ*, 182-83.

8. Mary Daly, *Beyond God the Father: Toward a Philosophy of Women's Liberation* (Boston: Beacon Press, 1973), 73-74; Heyward, *Passion*, 29.

9. Heyward, *Passion*, 214.

10. Cited in Anne E. Carr, *Transforming Grace: Christian Tradition and Women's Experience* (San Francisco: Harper & Row, 1988), 160.

11. Susan B. Thistlethwaite, *Sex, Race and God: Christian Feminism in Black and White* (New York: Crossroad, 1989), 94-95.

12. Rosemary R. Ruether, "Christology and Feminism: Can a Male Saviour Save Women?" in Rosemary R. Ruether, *To Change the World: Christology and Cultural Criticism* (New York: Crossroad, 1981), 47.

13. "Document 10. Jarena Lee: Black Women Wrestle with the 'Call to Preach the Gospel,' " in *In Our Own Voices: Four Centuries of American Women's Religious Writing*, ed. Rosemary S. Keller and Rosemary R. Ruether (San Francisco: HarperSanFrancisco, 1995), 335.

14. Elizabeth A. Johnson, "Redeeming the Name of Christ," in *Freeing Theology: The Essentials of Theology in Feminist Perspective*, ed. Catherine M. LaCugna (San Francisco: HarperSanFrancisco, 1993), 118-19.

15. Johnson, "Redeeming the Name of Christ," 126.

16. Ibid., 127.

17. Ruether, "Christology and Feminism," 56.

18. Mexico Conference, "Final Document on Doing Theology from a Third World Women's Perspective," in *Feminist Theology from the Third World*, ed. Ursula King (Maryknoll: Orbis Books, 1994), 40.

19. Heyward, *Passion*, 216.

20. Thoko Mpumlwana, "My Perspective on Women and Their Role in Church and Society," King, *Feminist Theology*, 167.

21. Grant, *White Women's Christ*, 217.

22. Virginia Fabella, "A Common Method for Diverse Christologies?" in *With Passion and Compassion: Third World Women Doing Theology*, ed. Virginia Fabella and Mercy A. Oduyoye (Maryknoll: Orbis Books, 1988), 113.

23. Julian of Norwich, *Showings*, tr. Edmund Colledge and James Walsh (New York: Paulist Press, 1978), 298-301.

24. For another example of feminine imagery for Jesus, see Elizabeth A. Johnson's discussion of wisdom, usually personified as female, in *She Who Is: The Mystery of God in Feminist Theological Discourse* (New York: Crossroad, 1994), 86-100.

25. Brian Wren, *What Language Shall I Borrow? God-Talk in Worship: A Male Response to Feminist Theology* (New York: Crossroad, 1991), 171.

26. Ibid., 181.

6. Salvation

1. Sheri Reynolds, *The Rapture of Canaan* (New York: Berkley Books, 1995).

2. The text claims to be a letter written by Paul to his young friend Timothy; but because of the differing vocabulary and assumptions about church offices, many scholars believe that the letter was not written by Paul, but by someone late in the first or early in the second century. This helps to explain why the attitude toward women seems rather different from other Pauline letters.

3. See the discussion of Martin Luther's and John Calvin's exegesis of this text in Rosemary R. Ruether, *Women and Redemption: A Theological History* (Minneapolis: Fortress Press, 1998), 117-26.

4. Thomas C. Oden, *First and Second Timothy and Titus,* Interpretation Commentary (Louisville: Westminster/John Knox Press, 1989), 99-102.

5. See the commentary on 1 Timothy by Joanna Dewey in *The Women's Bible Commentary,* ed. Carol A. Newsom and Sharon H. Ringe (Louisville: Westminster/John Knox Press, 1992), 353-58.

6. Rosemary R. Ruether, "Misogynism and Virginal Feminism in the Fathers of the Church," in *Religion and Sexism* (New York: Simon and Schuster, 1974), 150-83.

7. Mary Daly, *Beyond God the Father: Toward a Philosophy of Women's Liberation* (Boston: Beacon Press, 1973), 65.

8. See Mary Pipher, *Reviving Ophelia: Saving the Selves of Adolescent Girls* (New York: Ballantine Books, 1995); and Carol L. Hess, "Reclaiming Ourselves: A Spirituality for Women's Empowerment," *Women, Gender, and Community,* ed. Jane D. Douglass and James F. Kay (Louisville: Westminster/John Knox Press, 1997).

9. Judith Plaskow, *Sex, Sin and Grace: Women's Experience and the Theologies of Reinhold Niebuhr and Paul Tillich* (Washington, D.C.: University Press of America, 1980), 85.

10. Roberta C. Bondi, *Memories of God: Theological Reflections on a Life* (Nashville: Abingdon Press, 1995), 121.

11. Daphne Hampson, *Theology and Feminism* (Cambridge, Mass.: Basil Blackwell, 1990), 127.

12. Delores Williams, "A Womanist Perspective on Sin," and Jacquelyn Grant, "The Sin of Servanthood and the Deliverance of Discipleship," in *A Troubling in My Soul: Womanist Perspectives on Evil and Suffering,* ed. Emilie Townes, (Maryknoll: Orbis Books, 1993), 147, 215.

13. Julian of Norwich, *Revelations of Divine Love,* tr. Clifton Walters (New York: Penguin Books, 1966), 152.

14. Mary D. Pellauer with Susan B. Thistlethwaite, "Conversation on Grace and Healing: Perspectives from the Movement to End Violence Against Women," in *Lift Every Voice: Constructing Christian Theology from the Underside,* ed. Susan B. Thistlethwaite and Mary P. Engel (New York: HarperSanFrancisco, 1990), 181.

15. Sheri Reynolds, *The Rapture of Canaan,* 316.

16. Judith R. Wegner, "Leviticus," in *The Women's Bible Commentary,* 36.

17. Joanne C. Brown and Rebecca Parker, "For God So Loved the World?" in *Christianity, Patriarchy and Abuse: A Feminist Critique,* ed. Joanne C. Brown and Carole R. Bohn (New York: Pilgrim Press, 1989), 23.

18. Nancy Mairs, *Ordinary Time: Cycles in Marriage, Faith, and Renewal* (Boston: Beacon Press, 1993), 138.

19. Rita N. Brock, *Journeys by Heart: A Christology of Erotic Power* (New York: Crossroad, 1988), 93.

20. Ibid., 86, 105.

21. Brown and Parker, "For God So Loved the World?" 2.

22. Delores Williams, *Sisters in the Wilderness: The Challenge of Womanist God-Talk* (Maryknoll: Orbis Books, 1993), 167.

23. Ellen K. Wondra, *Humanity Has Been a Holy Thing: Toward a Contemporary Feminist Christology* (Lanham, Md.: University Press of America, 1994), 333.

24. Therese Souga, "The Christ-Event from the Viewpoint of African Women, I. A Catholic Perspective," in *With Passion and Compassion: Third World Women Doing Theology*, ed. Virginia Fabella and Mercy A. Oduyoye (Maryknoll: Orbis Books, 1988), 28.

25. Mary A. O'Neill, "The Mystery of Being Human Together," in *Transforming Grace*, ed. Catherine M. LaCugna (New York: HarperSanFrancisco, 1993), 145.

26. Virginia Fabella, "A Common Methodology for Diverse Christologies," in *With Passion and Compassion*, 111.

27. Letty M. Russell, *Human Liberation in Feminist Perspective* (Philadelphia: Westminster Press, 1974), 153.

28. Sally Purvis, *The Power of the Cross: Foundations for a Christian Feminist Ethic of Community* (Nashville: Abingdon Press, 1993), 74-75.

29. Ibid., 77.

30. Ibid., 88.

31. Ibid., 88-89.

32. Jean Zaru, "The Intifada, Nonviolence, and the Bible," in *Feminist Theology from the Third World: A Reader*, ed. Ursula King (Maryknoll: Orbis Books, 1994), 232.

33. Leanne Van Dyk, "Do Theories of Atonement Foster Abuse?" *Perspectives*, February 1997, 13.

7. Church and Ministry

1. Reprinted in *Women and Religion in America*, vol. 1, *The Nineteenth Century*, ed. Rosemary R. Ruether and Rosemary S. Keller (San Francisco: Harper & Row, 1981), 40.

2. "Document 10. Jarena Lee: Black Women Wrestle with the 'Call to Preach the Gospel,' " in *In Our Own Voices: Four Centuries of American Women's Religious Writing*, ed. Rosemary S. Keller and Rosemary R. Ruether (San Francisco: HarperSanFrancisco, 1995), 335.

3. Rosemary R. Ruether, *Women-Church: Theology and Practice of Feminist Liturgical Communities* (San Francisco: HarperSanFrancisco, 1985), 4-5.

4. Rosemary Edet and Bette Ekeya, "Church Women of Africa: A Theological Community," in *With Passion and Compassion: Third World Women Doing Theology,* ed. Virginia Fabella and Mercy A. Oduyoye (Maryknoll: Orbis Books, 1988), 4.

5. Mary Daly, *The Church and the Second Sex* (New York: Harper & Row, 1968), 202-3.

6. Gerrit Vander Lugt, ed., *Liturgy and Psalms* (New York: The Board of Education, 1968), 97.

7. Mary Daly, "The Women's Movement: An Exodus Community," *Religious Education* 67 (Sept./Oct. 1972): 327-33. Reprinted in *Women and Religion: The Original Sourcebook of Women in Christian Thought,* ed. Elizabeth A. Clark and Herbert W. Richardson (San Francisco: HarperSanFrancisco, 1996), 317-18.

8. Mary Daly, *Beyond God the Father: Toward a Philosophy of Women's Liberation* (Boston: Beacon Press, 1973), 143.

9. Joanne C. Brown and Rebecca Parker, "For God So Loved the World?" in *Christianity, Patriarchy and Abuse: A Feminist Critique,* ed. Joanne C. Brown and Carole R. Bohn (New York: Pilgrim Press, 1989), 3.

10. Letty M. Russell, *Church in the Round: Feminist Interpretation of the Church* (Louisville: Westminster/John Knox Press, 1993), 25.

11. Daly, *The Church and the Second Sex,* 83.

12. Elisabeth S. Fiorenza, *Discipleship of Equals: A Critical Feminist Ekklesia-logy of Liberation* (New York: Crossroad, 1993), 92.

13. Ibid., 131.

14. Ibid., 102.

15. Ibid., 150.

16. Miriam T. Winter, Adair Lummis, and Allison Stokes, *Defecting in Place: Women Taking Responsibility for Their Own Spiritual Lives* (New York: Crossroad, 1994).

17. For a description of WomenChurch groups and some of their rituals, see Rosemary R. Ruether, *Women-Church.*

18. Clark and Richardson, *Women and Religion,* 86-87.

19. *Boswell's Life of Johnson,* ed. George B. Hill (London: Oxford University Press, 1934), 1:463.

20. Ruether, *Women-Church,* 81.

21. Anna G. Spencer, "Woman's Share in Social Culture," *Feminism: The Essential Historical Writings,* ed. Miriam Schneir (New York: Vintage Books, 1972), 284.